The
miracles
of Christ

The
miracles
of Christ

and what they mean
to you for ALL your needs
in the now

by Oral Roberts

FIRST PUBLISHED EDITION

FIRST PRINTING	100,000	MARCH 1975
SECOND PRINTING	200,000	APRIL 1975
THIRD PRINTING	200,000	MAY 1975

CONTENTS

Oral Roberts

1

THE MIRACLE
CHRIST OFFERS YOUR MARRIAGE AND
FAMILY IN TODAY'S WORLD

IT IS REALLY GREAT to know that Jesus performed His first miracle in a home. He was at a family gathering. He was personally interested in a young couple who was getting married. JESUS WAS THERE. Now that says a lot. In fact, it says something very important to you and me. He was there in a *home*. He was there with a *young couple*. He was there with the parents and their friends. Jesus was there in the midst of a wedding celebration . . . He was there in their joy. And when they ran out of wine and things were plunged into chaos, Jesus was *still* there.

As I said, that says a lot. Because Jesus is *here* just as He was there. Jesus is here. He's in your home. Everybody lives in some kind of home. Usually he lives with one or more persons.

Sometimes he lives alone. No matter. Jesus is where you are.

If you have a family He is present with each of them.

Jesus is still present at a marriage.

Jesus Christ is immeasurably interested in, and concerned about, your marriage and my marriage. Whether your marriage has already happened, as mine has, or is about to happen—Jesus is concerned and cares.

HERE IN THIS FIRST MIRACLE WE SEE MAR-RIAGE IS SOMETHING THAT CAPTURED JESUS' ATTENTION AND TO WHICH HE GAVE HIS DEEPEST CONCERN. A MARRIAGE CELEBRA-TION BROUGHT ABOUT HIS PRESENCE—JESUS WAS THERE.

Everything was going well at the wedding until they ran out of wine. In those days wine was an integral part of the wedding feast. To run out was embarrassing and brought about confusion. Suddenly they were in trouble.

It's exactly like what happens to you and to me in our homes, in our families, and in our relationships. It's what the business world calls Murphy's Law. Murphy's Law says, "If anything bad can happen, it will." I am with all kinds of people and many times I'm with individuals who, whether they know it or not, are practicing Murphy's Law. They believe that if anything bad can happen, it will. This kind of thinking has an insidious way of working its way into our thoughts until we develop an attitude whereby we not only expect bad things to happen to us but we also attract them. It becomes a magnifying force to bring bad things to our lives. Murphy's Law is very real to a great many people in this world. But there is a better way—Jesus' way.

Jesus was there . . . and He is here . . . But He does not accept Murphy's Law. He brought a new kind of law—His own law. Jesus says, "If anything good can happen, I'm going to bring it to pass." For example:

> *Every good gift and every perfect gift is from above, and cometh down from the Father of lights, with whom is no variableness, neither shadow of turning* (James 1:17).

Now Jesus is in the midst of a situation that is turning bad but He is there to turn it around, to enter into it—to bring himself into the humanness of their situation.

Jesus was there.

He was there in their humanness.

He was there in their loss.

He was there when the wine ran out.

HE WAS THERE TO SHOW THEM GOD'S WAY OF DOING THINGS! He was there to show them that if they would *learn His way of doing things and do it,* they could put things right again. Whatever was wrong would be restored. Whatever was diminished would be replenished.

And JESUS CHRIST IS HERE! He is wanting to teach you and me His way of doing things. I believe if you can learn to do things the way Jesus does them, then you'll be able to turn the bad things around that happen to you. There will be times you will be able to say, "My cup runneth over. . ."

There are three things that happened in this miracle that are *terribly* important to you in the NOW:

1. JESUS BROUGHT MANKIND A NEW KIND OF RELATIONSHIP WITH GOD, A VERY PERSONAL RELATIONSHIP

The first thing Jesus did in the miracle of turning the water into wine at Cana of Galilee was to give each person a new kind of relationship with God. Let me explain. In the Old Testament, the first miracle Moses performed was before Pharaoh in Egypt, where Israel was in bondage. There Moses turned water into blood—a symbol of destruction and death. The first miracle our Lord Jesus performed was to turn the same kind of water into *wine*—a symbol of life, joy, and happiness.

Another example: The Old Testament ends with a book called Malachi which is the prophecy of the Prophet Malachi. By that time in history the children of Israel had become so disobedient that God was very upset with them. In the final verses of this book God calls upon them to repent and to change, lest He come and smite the earth with a curse.

THE OLD TESTAMENT ENDS WITH THE THREAT OF A CURSE—THE NEW TESTAMENT BEGINS WITH THE BIRTH OF A BABY AND THE PROMISE OF LIFE.

In Matthew 1:21 we read:

> *Thou shall call his name* JESUS: *for he shall save his people from their sins.*

And the angels sang:

> *For unto you is born this day in the city of David a Saviour, which is Christ the Lord . . . on earth peace, good will toward men* (Luke 2:11,14).

JESUS WAS NOT ONLY A SAVIOR FROM SIN BUT HE WAS ALSO A SAVIOR OF *PERSONS*. The word *saved* in those days was the same root word for heal. So this verse really means:

> You shall call His name Jesus for He shall heal persons. He shall heal them from their sins, their shortcomings, their failures, the disharmony of their nature. He shall heal their bodies. He shall heal their minds. He shall heal their whole beings . . . that's why His name shall be called Jesus.

When Jesus came the world was still in rebellion. The children of Israel were still in disobedience. They were still under the threat of a curse. This included the whole earth.

But . . .

JESUS' PRESENCE CHANGES THINGS.
He offers a blessing rather than a curse . . .
healing rather than sickness . . .
a supply for your needs rather than an imposition of poverty.

Jesus came to break the poverty cycle, the sickness cycle, the sin cycle. He came to bring the cycle of wholeness to your life.

This is the new relationship Jesus Christ came to bring between himself and you. It is actually a New Covenant.

The Old Testament means "Old Covenant or Contract." New Testament means "New Covenant or New Contract." God has made a New Contract. The Old Contract has now served its purpose. Now a New Covenant is superimposed upon it. The Covenant contains not the threat of a curse, but the promise of a blessing . . . not that the water will be turned into blood, but into wine . . . not that God is going to trap you and destroy you, but instead God is there with His everlasting love and mercy to save you—to heal your life, your whole being.

This is what changed my life. Growing up I had a hard time trying to comprehend that God even existed, let alone trying to understand Him. As a child, even if you grow up in a religious home you find it's difficult to understand God. As a little boy I was frightened of God. I was actually afraid that He would slam me into hell. I think that was part of my rebellion I developed over my teen-age years. Out of this rebellion I left my family. I left the church. I ran away from home to go my own way and I lost my health. I developed tuberculosis. I was brought home to my parents. I could no longer run away because I had no strength and no money. I was a captive. Many Christian people told me that God had put the illness on me.

After five months of being bedfast I had a bitterness in me about God. I hope you never develop that because it almost destroyed my life. But, you know, Jesus was there and He brought me into a new personal relationship with himself. It happened through my sister Jewel. She walked in one day, looked at my wasted body, and said:

"Oral, God is going to heal you."

Just seven simple words . . . but immediately I saw God in a new light. I don't mean I saw Him with my eyes but I understood in my inner self that God is not like I thought He was, or like I had been led to believe that He is. Almost in an instant it dawned on me that God is good . . . He is concerned—*even* about me.

I'm in a position of some prominence today. I know that. It's so different from what I was when I was not known—when I was just known as a preacher's kid, the boy who had run away and was brought back home to die. I lived in a little country town of a few hundred people. I was the son of a minister. We were so poor the poor people called us poor. And there I lay bedfast, with tuberculosis. There was no prominence about that, my friend. There was no evidence of a worldwide ministry or the building of a university. The evidence was:

I was hemorrhaging to death.

When I tried to talk, I stammered.

I needed a new relationship with God, a personal relationship.

Three fine doctors helped me. They worked hard but that was before the so-called miracle drugs. They could do very little for people with tuberculosis. In the hills of eastern Oklahoma—Talihina—is a sanatorium for people with tuberculosis. I was scheduled to go there when my sister said, "Oral, God is going to heal you."

And, do you know, I fell in love with God. I thought, anybody who would care enough to help me must be wonderful. I believe . . .

GOD COMES TO EVERYBODY–SOMEHOW!

God may not come to you exactly like He came to me, but there is some way He will come to you—in a way you can understand if you try.

God turned "water into wine" for me.

He turned my lungs into proper breathing and my stammering tongue into normal talking.

I thank God for His healing power because it is through it that I breathe and talk today. I am thankful for God's healing love and power and I tell you, friend, God is still turning water into wine. He's still giving individuals a new relationship with himself. He is still healing people like yourself. And he will keep on doing it. Learn how He does it and get into the healing stream.

2. JESUS CHRIST BROUGHT A NEW TYPE OF MIRACLE–THE MIRACLE OF SEED-FAITH, THE MIRACLE OF REPRODUCING WHAT YOU GIVE TO HIM

Miracles were in evidence from time to time during Old Testament days. God performed miracles of supply where there was little or no supply. At times God would multiply something that was completely running out, as He multiplied the wasting meal and oil of the widow of Zarephath (1 Kings 17: 8-16). Or when there was nothing to eat, God sent manna down from heaven for the children of Israel—"a miracle out of the blue," we might say. These miracles were very practical and down to earth and saved a person's life or extended his life into better things.

Now God did some miracles in Old Testament times but miracles were not a regular thing. They were virtually unknown as a regular occurrence until our Lord Jesus Christ came and as His first miracle, turned the water into wine. Let me explain by recapturing what was happening at the wedding feast. They ran out of wine and Jesus' mother, Mary, turned to Him and said, "Son, they've run out of wine."

Now Mary could have consoled the host but, no, she did not do this. She knew the Source of all blessings and she went to Him—Jesus. She went confident of His love and she informed Him of the problem.

Jesus replied something like this, "Mother, it's not quite time for Me to begin My public ministry . . . not at this point. What does their running out of wine have to do with Me?"

Mary was not discouraged by Jesus' statement. If it had been me, I might have said, "Lord, please forgive me for bothering You. I had hoped that You might do something but I can see that it's not the proper time . . . that it is not Your will to take care of this particular situation . . . it would upset Your timetable. I'm sincerely sorry that I mentioned it to You."

Mary does not say this because by now she *knows* who her Son is. So she turns to the servants and says, "Whatever Jesus says to you, you do it."

This is the unconquerable faith Mary had in Jesus. It is also the knowledge she had of His way of doing things. Mary knew when Jesus did something, He did it the way it should be done. And . . .

MARY KNEW IF PEOPLE WOULD LEARN TO DO THINGS JESUS' WAY . . .

that which was beyond human comprehension could be comprehended . . .

that which was humanly impossible would become possible.

The unseen would be seen.

The unreal would become real.

God would be there as if He were in the flesh. (Of course through Jesus Christ, God in that moment *was* there in the flesh.)

It is interesting to note that Mary left the means of solving the "no-more-wine problem" to Jesus. She did not say, "Please, Jesus, cause the guests to go home." Or, "Cause them to be satisfied with the wine they've drunk because there is no more." She simply stated the problem and left the means of solving it to Jesus. He was the Source, and Mary believed in "due season" Jesus would do it in His own *time* and *way.*

JUST REMEMBER JESUS IS THE SOURCE AND AS THE SOURCE HE IS NOT LIMITED TO PERFORMING ONLY ONE TYPE OF MIRACLE.

He can change substances.

He can transcend all difficulties.

He can create.

He can recreate.

He can multiply that which is given to Him.

God can and does send miracles to us in many ways.

At the marriage in Cana Jesus asked them to give what they had—water. He asked them to give out of their need, to sow what they had. There was no more wine but Jesus directed the servants to sow *water.* They did so with all the obedience of which they were capable and they were rewarded in direct proportion to what they had sown.

Now we accept some transformations as being natural, such as an acorn becoming a giant oak or a caterpillar becoming a butterfly. Still it requires faith to plant an acorn and expect an oak tree. And it still requires a genuine faith in God as the Source of all things to obey Him when He tells us to fill the waterpots (or to give of what we have).

> IT REQUIRES FAITH TO BELIEVE GOD CAN CHANGE WATER INTO WINE . . . AND OUR OWN PERSONAL NEED INTO AN ABUNDANT SUPPLY.

> IT TAKES FAITH BECAUSE IT GOES AGAINST ALL HUMAN REASONING.

> IT GOES AGAINST EVERYTHING OUR MIND HAS BEEN TAUGHT BY MAN'S REASON.

But Jesus said to the servants, "You see those large water pots; I want you to fill them with water."

The servants did that.

Then Jesus said, "Now, pour it out and take a glass to the governor of the feast."

Don't you think that's a bit strange for a human being to do? Don't you think that goes against all rationality? Against all logic that you learned in school? Don't you think that rather defies your imagination? Don't you think that if you had faced that personally with the Lord Jesus, you would have had some difficulty in accepting or trying to comprehend what He said? Jesus said, "You put it in and then you take it out. I want you to do what I tell you to do. First, I want your obedience. I want you to learn My way of doing things."

> GOD HAS A CERTAIN WAY OF DOING THINGS.
> WHEN WE GET IN THE STREAM OF THE WAY

HE DOES THINGS, WE'RE FLOWING WITH THE STREAM AND THE STREAM IS FLOWING WITH US. WE'RE IN A WHOLE NEW DIMENSION OF LIFE . . . THE MIRACLE REALM.

The important thing is to give whatever the Lord lays on your heart to give and give it first. Give it even though it looks foolish . . . even though you can't understand how giving something of what you have is going to be multiplied to help meet your great need. Remember the miracle of Seed-Faith says:

GIVE GOD SOMETHING TO WORK WITH

The rational mind has a difficult time trying to grasp this; whereas down deep within us is this intuitive power, the Spirit of the Lord working upon our spirit. Down deep within us is The Force and we who use it know that it often defies the rational mind. It is in our spirit that we first respond to God.

Now the rational mind has to be willing to take a step of faith and risk something. *Risk something*. What these servants were risking was to look foolish. The Man said, "Fill up the waterpots." Then He said, "Pour it out."

The servants demonstrated *obedience* and a *measure of faith*. After all, they would leave themselves open to possible ridicule and rebuke if they handed the head waiter a glass of plain water to taste. Yet they obeyed.

When the servants poured the water out, its nature was transformed and multiplied . . . it had become *WINE*. It was an unheard-of miracle.

Jesus was later to speak of miracles as doing "the works" of His Father. Although the writers of the Gospels freely used the word *miracle,* Jesus seldom did. Rather, He called His miracles "the works of my father" (John 10:37, 38).

Here Jesus was able to bring *the works of the Father* down to a personal level for meeting individual needs in immediate circumstances. Jesus *concentrated* into single moments the things that the Father had been doing over long periods of time, such as the growth of grapes for wine, the process of fermentation and all that goes into the making of wine. **Jesus telescoped time and brought this miracle into the NOW of their needs.** This destroys the argument that God does not do miracles anymore since that would be breaking His own natural laws. But Jesus didn't break the laws of nature, He simply intervened and caused the process to happen instantly which normally would have taken a long time.

The governor of the feast tasted the wine and he was immediately impressed because it tasted better than the other wine. He said, "It's rather strange what you people are doing. Usually the host doesn't save the best wine for the last. He serves it first. Then when people have well drunk they don't know whether it's good or bad, so he serves the lesser wine. Here you've done exactly the opposite. You've served the worst first. And you're serving the best last."

> IT WAS A MIRACLE OF TRANSFORMATION. IT WAS THE TRANSFORMATION OF ONE LIQUID – WATER – INTO A LIQUID THAT WAS ALTOGETHER DIFFERENT—WINE. IT WAS THE TRANSFORMATION AND MULTIPLICATION OF THEIR *WANT* INTO *AN ABUNDANT SUPPLY! IT WAS THE MIRACLE OF SEED-FAITH.*

Had Jesus multiplied the water, it still would not have met their need. They needed *wine!* Jesus took the thing they had—water (which represented their great need)—and transformed it into wine (abundant supply)! Wine was their need and Jesus always meets you at the point of your need.

The whole miracle of the turning of the water into wine was a result of a series of giving.

First, Mary had given Jesus to the world as "the seed of David" (John 7:42). Mary offered up herself to God in an act of supreme obedience . . . giving herself as a young virgin . . . being willing to be stoned, which was sentence put upon a person who would be classified as an adultress in that day. She was willing to face anything to give our Lord to the world (Luke 1:26-38).

Second, Mary is giving priceless information to these distraught people, telling them how Jesus does things. Mary is in a state of giving . . . giving lovingly and cheerfully. And giving FIRST.
She is in a state of giving something to God to work with. She is in the process of *seed-planting*.

Third, the servants start giving. What were they out of? Wine. Now they were told to take some liquid and put it in. And they obeyed. They poured in the water. This goes all the way back to Genesis 8:22: *While the earth remaineth, seedtime and harvest . . . shall not cease.*

That is, there will be sowing and reaping as long as the earth remains. There will be *giving* and *receiving*. In Luke 6:38, our Lord enlarges upon this. He said:

> *Give, and it shall be given unto you; good measure, pressed down, and shaken together, and running over, shall men give into your bosom. For with the*

*same measure that ye [give] withal it shall be
measured to you again.*

You talk about a critical situation! This family was out
of the one thing that made a feast a success—wine! In our
day we would say the bottom of the economy had dropped
out . . . that inflation had gotten so bad they couldn't make
it. We might say it this way: "Bills are piling up and I can't
meet them. Everything has gone wrong."

Some say, "What have I done to deserve this? Why has
this happened to me?"

Someone else says, "I hate to read the newspaper because the bad news distresses me."

Another person puts on a long face, as though God
were dead, and says, "I can't make it."

That's the way these people felt at the wedding feast
at Cana of Galilee. But Jesus was there and He simply said,
"Give something first—put something in."

Does this pass over your head? **Mary gave us the first
key principle of Seed-Faith:**

GOD IS THE SOURCE OF YOUR TOTAL SUPPLY!

She said, "Whatsoever *Christ* says unto you, you do it."
In other words, "The answer to this crisis here in Cana of
Galilee is in this Man Jesus Christ. He's the Source of your
supply for what you've run out of."

I believe in banks. I borrow from banks but in no way
can I trust banks to be my source of supply. For if I do,
they may refuse me money the day I need it the most. All
of their excuses and all their saying, "Mr. Roberts, I'm sorry
. . . " won't help me a bit. If I go away with a "no" it's still
a "no." Even though they smile when they say it, it hurts
me just as bad. My pockets are still empty. So I've got to
look to God as my banker. The bank may, or may not, be

able to help me but my God will always help me if I trust Him as my Source. He will make a way where there is no way.

I may take my marriage to a marriage counselor but in no way is that marriage counselor my source. He or she can be a fine instrument for God to use but God is the Source of keeping my marriage intact. In every part of my existence God is my Source.

Mary said, *Whatever He says unto you, do it.*

These servants *seeded* for their miracle. They put the seed in. They poured the water in. They gave of something that they could give—they sowed water. **This is the second key principle of Seed-Faith, seeding for your miracle and doing it first.**

GOD NEVER ASKS YOU TO GIVE SOMETHING YOU CANNOT GIVE

Sometimes He asks for something so small you are embarrassed to give it. I often tell people who start in Seed-Faith, "Don't start with something big . . . *start with something small.* Let God show you what He will do and then increase it, because you'll be able to increase it. But start with something—no matter how small."

I believe you should start with something like these people did, something commonplace. In this case—water. The wine was gone but they had water. So they gave—they put in the seed.

After the servants had obeyed . . . after they had given . . . they expected a miracle. How do we know they did? The Bible says when the governor of the feast poured the water out he didn't *know* what had happened, but the servants *knew.* They KNEW. They knew a miracle was happening because now they've gotten caught up in what

Jesus had told them to do. They had learned to do what He had told them to do. They had learned His way of doing things and they had done it. They'd gotten into a terrific state of expectancy. The Bible indicates THEY KNEW . . . THEY *EXPECTED* . . . AND THE MIRACLE HAPPENED RIGHT IN FRONT OF THEM. **This is the third key principle of Seed-Faith: Expect A Miracle!**

There is a man in the city of Tulsa who is a successful businessman but a very modest, unassuming person. He is a deeply committed Christian man. We became close friends and my admiration for him grew so much until one day I said, "How did you meet our Lord? How did Christ become real to you?"

He said, "I found Him through my giving."

I said, "How did you do that?"

"Well," he said, "for years I could not comprehend God at all. Then one day I read a book written by Lloyd Douglas, entitled *Magnificent Obsession*. This book is about a young man who had a lot of money, but who had wasted his life and was finally involved in an accident. After the accident he made a commitment to give himself to God and to start giving. Most of his giving was anonymous. He didn't want people to know he had given to them. He spent his life doing this. It became a *magnificent obsession* to him."

Then my friend said, "I, too, began to quietly give. Most of the time it was anonymous. One day I became aware that I felt the presence of God. More and more, God became real to me." Then he said, "Oral, the most real person in my life today is God."

This friend is a man that I cannot allow myself to see very often because he wants to give me something every time I see him. This is dangerous because if you know this about a person, you're going to want to see him more often.

This can get you into all kinds of problems. First of all, you'll be tempted to make him a source. The moment you make anybody your source you are in trouble. You've got to keep it on a higher level, that God is your Source, and everyone else or everything else is an instrument only.

Now we come to the third important point in this miracle that is very important to you.

3. JESUS CHRIST TELLS US . . . A MIRACLE REALLY IS ANOTHER ONE OF THE WORKS OF GOD

Now this is terribly important and I'm going to tell you why. In Chapter 2, the 11th verse of John, it says:

> *This beginning of miracles did Jesus . . .*

This beginning of miracles. The word *beginning* means Jesus started something which He meant to continue. Then the word *miracle* was used. I want you to get this fact: Only once did Jesus refer to miracles and that is found in John 6:26. The rest of the time He referred to miracles as the works of God or the works of the Father. Now Matthew, Mark, Luke, and John continually said Christ performed *miracles*. In fact, John, who wrote the story of the turning of the water into wine, said, "This beginning of miracles did Jesus. . ." John used the word *miracle*. But Jesus called miracles the works of God. For example:

> *Then answered Jesus and said unto them, Verily, verily, I say unto you, The Son can do nothing of himself, but what he seeth the Father do . . . (John 5:19).*

That is, whatever Jesus did is what He had seen the Father do. Jesus was the essential nature of God himself. He came to show us what God is like. He came to do what God does, but to do it on a human plane so we could grasp it. He,

Jesus, is saying that He does nothing of himself. He does only what He has seen the Father do.

> For the works which the Father hath given me to finish, the same works that I do, bear witness of me, that the Father hath sent me (John 5:36).

In other words, Jesus said, "I do the works of my Father."

Then in John 9:4, Jesus said:

> I must work the works of him that sent me.

Jesus is talking about doing the works of God. WORKS OF GOD. In John 10:37,38, Jesus said:

> If I do not the works of my Father, believe me not. But if I do, though ye believe not me, believe the works . . .

In essence, Jesus was saying, "If you cannot believe that I am the Son of God, believe these works—these works of God."

Jesus is still talking about the works of God in Luke 4:18 when He says:

> The Spirit of the Lord is upon me, because he hath anointed me to preach the gospel to the poor.

He was really saying, "God has sent me with good news to the poor—YOU DON'T HAVE TO BE POOR ANYMORE."

> He hath sent me to heal the brokenhearted, to preach deliverance to the captives, and recovering of sight to the blind, to set at liberty them that are bruised, to preach the acceptable year of the Lord.

These are the WORKS Jesus is doing. These are the works of the Father. These are what the gospel writers call miracles (or wonders).

Today there's a tremendous theological question which has not been resolved by millions of Christians and that is, have miracles ceased? Many admit the miracles of 2,000 years ago but they question, "Can miracles happen today? Is the essential nature of God to perform miracles the same now as it was then?"

Jesus indicates a miracle is not a sometime or onetime thing. It is not some sort of magic. He places a miracle in the category of the *works of God*. Now the moment you stop calling them miracles and put them into the area of the works of God, then you see that Jesus Christ has only come to do what God has been doing all through the centuries and will do forever. Jesus came to do the works of the Father. He is carrying out the essential nature of His Father which is to bring His works of LIFE to the world. He explains here that the Spirit of God is upon Him and He's come to do these mighty works of the Father.

Acts 10:38 says:

> *God anointed Jesus of Nazareth with the Holy Ghost and with power: who went about doing good, and healing all that were oppressed of the devil; for God was with him.*

First Jesus was anointed with the Holy Spirit. Then He went about doing good and healing all that were oppressed of the devil, for God was with Him. He was doing the WORKS OF GOD. If you're turned off by the word *miracles*, don't worry about it. Call them the works of God. Jesus did not deny that they were miracles, but He emphasized that these miracles were really the works of God.

In 1 Corinthians 12:10, we learn that one of the nine gifts of the Spirit is the working of miracles. The *working* of them. Here again are WORKS. The works of our Father.

In John 14:12, we read:

> *Greater works than these shall [ye] do; because I go unto my Father.*

Greater WORKS shall ye do.

In Acts 3 the story is told of how the apostles brought healing to the lame man who was carried daily and placed at the gate of the Temple in Jerusalem. Peter and John came by one day and by faith the man was healed. Because of this healing they were persecuted. In fact, they were whipped.

> *And they called them, and commanded them not to speak at all nor teach in the name of Jesus. But Peter and John answered and said unto them, Whether it be right in the sight of God to hearken unto you more than unto God, judge ye. For we cannot but speak the things which we have seen and heard. So when they had further threatened them, they let them go, finding nothing how they might punish them, because of the people* (Acts 4:18-21).

The apostles returned unto their own company. And they prayed:

> *And now, Lord, behold their threatenings: and grant unto thy servants, that with all boldness they may speak thy word, by stretching forth thine hand to heal: and that signs and wonders may be done by the name of thy holy child Jesus* (Acts 4:29,30).

This is after the ascension of Christ. Christ is no longer on the earth in His flesh. He's been crucified and resurrected. He has now ascended back to His Father as the glorified Christ. His disciples are still doing the same works, even greater works. They are being persecuted for it. They've returned to pray and they call upon the Lord *not* to deliver them from persecution but to grant that they may speak His words with boldness by stretching forth His hand to heal . . . *by letting them continue to do the works of God.*

What I'm saying is this: This beginning of miracles, or *this beginning of the WORKS OF GOD, did our Lord.* It was not an *ending* of the works of God but a *beginning* of the works of God. These WORKS of God carried over into the lives of His followers. And they are in the lives of His followers today if we'll only accept them. If the word *miracle* is negative to you, dismiss it from your mind. Simply take the WORKS OF GOD and apply them to your personal life.

E. Stanley Jones, who is now with our Lord, was a famous Methodist missionary in India for some 50 years. He wrote many books. *The Christ of the Indian Road* is one of them. I'm sure many of you are familiar with his books. I'm told that sometime before his homegoing, when he was in his 80's, he had a stroke of paralysis. The doctors were able to help him in a Boston, Massachusetts hospital but not enough to make him walk. He asked his family to let him go back to India. There in India he called in many of the people whom he had led to Christ, who now were strong in the Lord. He said to them, "Open the Bible to the book of Acts, Chapter 3, where Peter and John said to the lame man, 'In the name of Jesus Christ, rise up and walk.' Now each morning I want you to come into my room before daylight, before I awaken, and whisper in my ear, 'In the name of Jesus Christ, rise up and walk.' "

They did as he asked. Then one day E. Stanley Jones felt a stirring in his body. He took his first step. Then other steps. Someone told him it was Columbus Day. Columbus Day celebrates the discovery of America by Christopher Columbus in 1492. On this particular day E. Stanley Jones felt God in a new way. He said, "I'm going to walk. In the name of Christ, I'm going to walk." As he walked, he counted his steps—1492 steps. E. Stanley Jones in his 80's, just prior to his going to be with the Lord, found the works of God were still working in him.

The meaning of this to you is rich and precious today. It means when you have insurmountable needs, needs that are so baffling and so terrible that they require something beyond the natural, beyond the ordinary, that you have recourse to God and His wonderful works. It means God can, and He *does,* come to you in the NOW.

IN SUMMARY I SAY TO YOU:

When our Lord turned the water into wine . . .

1. He offered to you a new personal relationship with God.
2. He offered to you a revolutionary but practical way to miracles—the miracle of Seed-Faith.
3. He offered to you HIS WORKS on a continuous basis. This means you can have not just a onetime or a sometime miracle . . . not something magic or hocus-pocus . . . but the actual WORKS OF GOD. And you can have the WORKS OF GOD in your life on a *continuous* basis . . . to restore your life . . . to replenish that which is getting away from you . . . to meet your bills that are piling up . . . to make you a WHOLE person . . . to meet ALL your needs.
4. He offered you the opportunity to learn His way of doing things so that you, too, can do the works of the Father to help meet the needs of other dear people, and to help yourself NOW.

2

THE MIRACLE
CHRIST OFFERS YOUR LOVED ONES

PERHAPS THE MIRACLE YOU NEED today isn't for yourself . . .
but it may be for a loved one who is in desperate straits
. . . or a son or daughter who is in trouble . . . or a friend
whose marriage is falling apart. Let me tell you, this work
of the Father that Jesus did in the healing of the nobleman's
son has a very, very special meaning for you in the NOW.
One of the great meanings of this miracle is . . .

JESUS COMES TO BOTH THE POOR AND THE RICH . . .
HE COMES TO US NO MATTER WHAT OUR
STATION IN LIFE IS

The second miracle—or work of the Father—Jesus did
also happened in Cana of Galilee . . . the same town in
which Jesus turned the water into wine. Now some time
has elapsed and He has returned. This time there is a man
who has arrived from the city of Capernaum. This man and
his family happen to be quite different from the family for
whom Jesus turned the water into wine. This man is a
nobleman. He represents wealth, position, prestige. In contrast, the other family was so poor they were unable to
afford enough wine for the marriage feast of their child.
Their money ran out . . . their wine ran out . . . so they had to
have a "miracle" to continue the feast.

On the one hand, we have a family who is depleted in their resources—who is diminished in their income, whose bills are piling up—and Jesus is concerned about them. On the other hand, we have a nobleman, a man with plenty of money, and Jesus is concerned for him and his need. I cannot overestimate this quality of mercy in our Lord Jesus Christ. It just means everything to everyone, that's all.

The nobleman came from Capernaum, which at that time was about a two-day trip from Cana. With the modern conveniences today you can go from Capernaum to Cana in perhaps one hour. But in that day it was possibly a two-day trip. It was a serious journey upon which the nobleman had embarked. His little son was at the point of death. And his cry was, "Sir, come down ere my child die."

And Jesus said to him, "Go thy way; thy son liveth."

We are told that the nobleman believed the words of our Lord. *He believed and he went home.* While he was journeying home some of his servants met him and told him that his child lived. He excitedly inquired about the time the child started to mend and they said, "At the seventh hour." That's when the nobleman KNEW. He knew that was the hour Jesus had said to him, "Go thy way; thy son liveth." It was out of this great work of the Father which Jesus did that the nobleman and his family established a life-pattern of believing. I want you to see the personal aspects of this miracle for you and your loved ones:

1. THE HEALING OF THE NOBLEMAN'S SON REMINDS YOU THAT OUR LORD JESUS CHRIST IS PERSON-CENTERED

Jesus is oriented toward the human being. We could say Jesus is oriented toward the human family and still be correct. But it's different when someone says, "God loves all the human family," than when he says, "God loves YOU." Both statements are true. God does love all people. But when that love is crystallized and individualized for your life it becomes infinitely more precious and desirable. It elevates the human individual above any institution, meaning that God does not institutionalize you by saying, "I will have My church open at 11 o'clock next Sunday morning and then I will take care of you as a person. I'll be there to give you My Word and to have prayers offered for you." It is true He will meet you at the house of the Lord. It is true we "should not forsake the assembling of ourselves together . . ." (Hebrews 10:25). But God does not institutionalize you in that way. He does not have a time of day when He begins doing business and certain hours when He says, "Now I can't work after hours."

GOD IS IN THE MIDST OF LIFE . . .
HE'S ALWAYS IN THE MIDST OF LIFE

God is in the midst of life. He is in the midst of *your life*. And you are more important to Him than even His universe. You are more important to Him than your car or your house or *anything* you possess. The key issue is: God is in the midst of *your* life and He values it above everything.

Do you recall the important incident in the life of our Savior when He was traveling with His disciples through a cornfield on the Sabbath day? His disciples were hungry. Having nothing to eat, they took the ears of corn and rubbed them in their hands so they could get the kernels (Luke 6:1). The enemies of our Lord, the Pharisees, being very religious but not spiritual (being outwardly pious but inwardly selfish and antisocial), said, "You've broken the Sabbath. Rubbing the ears of corn together constitutes work.

You are not to do any work on the Sabbath; therefore, you
have broken the Sabbath."

Jesus said, in essence, "Which one of you if he found
his ox in a ditch on the Sabbath would not go and get him
out?" (Luke 14:5). Then Jesus made this statement:

> *The sabbath was made for man, and not man for
> the sabbath* (Mark 2:27).

No greater statement was ever made by our Lord in
connection with His concern and care about you and me
as individuals. The great Sabbath day, with its rules and
regulations which dated back to the days of Moses, was
not greater than man. The hunger of these individuals was
more important to Jesus Christ than strict religious observance of the Law of Moses. In contrast, the Pharisees had
made the observance of the Law more important than life
itself.

**Jesus pointed out that man is more important than any
special religious day.** He said that every day is made for
man . . . including the Sabbath. The Sabbath is made for
man (Mark 2:27). Whatever accrues to man's benefit is
important, even though it might happen on a so-called
sacred day. In our Lord's view . . .

EVERY day is a holy day.

Every day is a day in which to enjoy life.

Every day is a day in which to have your needs
met.

Every day is a day to worship God.

Every day is a day in which you are the center
of HIS love and He is the center of yours.

Every day He's concerned about the details
of your existence, even numbering the hairs
on your head (Matthew 10:30).

Some three or four years ago I had something that I

had never experienced before. A kidney stone was forming in my body. I was filled with a pain that is indescribable. In fact, I thought I was going to die. Then I was scared I wasn't going to die. I mean, I hurt that bad.

While I was lying there on the bed trying to pray and trying to get some relief, my wife Evelyn was calling the Prayer Tower at the Oral Roberts University, and different friends on the campus, and everyone she could think of, asking them to pray. She also called Dr. Loveless. This dear man of God, a spirit-filled Methodist and our family doctor, came and immediately gave me an injection. Then he closed his little black medicine bag and looked at me. He looked at a human being, Oral Roberts. He was no longer looking at a patient, he was looking at a man who was hurting so bad he couldn't lie still. And I will never forget what he said. He said, "Brother Oral, would you let me pray for you?"

As I nodded, he didn't just sit on the side of my bed, he got up on the bed on his knees and he put his hands on me—the same hands that had just moments before administered medication. He put those hands upon me and looking up toward heaven, he said, "Jesus." Then he talked to Jesus like He was there in the room. He said, "Jesus, heal Your servant."

Now Dr. Loveless said other words in his prayer but that's all I can remember, because that was what I was interested in. He could have preached a sermon and I wouldn't have heard a word of it. I understood what he was saying, "Heal, Your servant." In a few moments I was asleep. I awakened about two hours later and I was well.

Later I was asked, "Which do you think healed you—the medicine Dr. Loveless gave you or the prayer he prayed?"

My reply was, "I don't know. It doesn't make any difference. I got well. I don't have the kidney stone anymore and I give the glory to God. If I was cured by the medicine, I thank God. If I was cured by the help of a medical doctor, I thank God. If I was healed by the power of his prayer to God, I thank God. Or if God used all of them in combination to heal me, I thank Him. I thank God for caring that much about me as a person. And I thank Him for permitting me to know Him as my Source."

I think in religion we have gotten so institutionalized we think of the *church* instead of the people who compose the church. In His second miracle our Lord is calling to our attention the value and importance of each man, woman, and child who has a need and that gloriously includes you and yours.

> JESUS CAN BE INTERRUPTED AT ANY TIME BECAUSE DOING THE WORKS OF THE FATHER IS NO INTERRUPTION TO HIM.

This is why Jesus came. He said, "I must work the works of him that sent me" (John 9:4). I think Jesus is trying to get across the idea that miracles are not to be so unusual. That is, the works of God are to be so *usual* that we should not be surprised when they happen. In fact, it should just be part of our normal order to ask for and receive the gifts of God—such as medicine, such as doctors, such as prayer and miracles.

2. THE MIRACLE OF THE HEALING OF THE NOBLEMAN'S SON TELLS YOU THERE IS NO DISTANCE IN YOUR FAITH

Distance was a problem in those days because they usually traveled by donkey. Capernaum is on the sea of

Galilee, while Cana is in the hills. It was a difficult trip but to add to the difficulty, a little child was at the point of death. Further complicating the matter is that this is a nobleman coming to a peasant preacher, Jesus Christ, and hoping He could heal his child. The nobleman was able to do all this except for one thing, his faith was based on Jesus Christ going to his home in person. He wanted Jesus to leave Cana and go to Capernaum . . . to leave the mountains and go to the seashore . . . to leave what He was doing in Cana of Galilee and go to Capernaum to the bedside of his child. The nobleman felt this was necessary in order for his faith to work for the child to be healed. So distance became a factor. Bridging the distance was part of a *source* to him.

The nobleman was simply living and believing the same way you and I too often do. He was living too much on the level of his five senses: seeing, hearing, tasting, touching, and smelling.

The nobleman wanted to *feel* the Lord's presence but only in the *place* and *way* he designated.

He wanted to *hear* the sound of His voice in the *place* and *way* he wanted to.

He wanted to be able to *see* the Lord bending over his child.

He wanted to experience Jesus Christ being there *physically* because his five senses were what he lived by.

Jesus Christ remonstrated with him saying, "Except ye see signs and wonders, ye will not believe" (John 4:48). Jesus was saying, "You are trying to confine Me, the Son of God, to the level of the five senses. While I am a physical, visible, limited man—having chosen to be that in order to enter into the humanness of every man—while I am the Son of man, *I am also the Son of God*. While I am able to heal in My physical presence and through the touch of My physical hands, I can also heal at a distance because I am God." In other words, "I can heal on a level *beyond* your five senses or on the sense level." Again I say it's very important for you and me to know this in the NOW of our needs.

Later on this became such a desperate situation in the lives of His followers that Jesus said:

> *Nevertheless I tell you the truth; It is expedient for you that I go away: for if I go not away, the Comforter* (Holy Spirit) *will not come unto you; but if I depart, I will send him unto you* (John 16:7).

Why did Jesus say this? Because Jesus knew in His humanity—having been born of the Virgin Mary, and becoming a man—He had to live on the level of the five senses. He was a limited, visible, physical human being who was subject to time, to death, and to space. He knew this could not continue always, that He could not be the *complete* Savior if He remained in the world in His physical body. Although Jesus dreaded death even as we do, He knew that He would have to die in order for His body to be raised from the dead and for Him to ascend back to His Father and be glorified. He knew this was necessary so He could go back to the original condition and position He had with His Father before the foundation of the earth was laid. There in His original glory, riches, and power, Jesus Christ could once again assume the position of the unseen or the invisible, unlimited God. When He had done this, then He would return in the power and the form of the Holy Spirit —His Other Self.

The Holy Spirit could not come in His invisible, unlimited presence as long as the visible, physical, limited presence of Jesus—the man—was upon the earth. His physical being had to be moved out. He had to get outside that human body. He had to be removed from it and be glorified in His new body. He himself—the inner man, the Christ Spirit—had to be removed from the body of Jesus, the man. Once that occurred and He was resurrected, ascended, and glorified, then He would pray the Father to send *another* Comforter—the Holy Spirit. Now, as I said, the Holy Spirit is Jesus' Other Self. Having the Holy Spirit is Jesus Christ himself abiding not only *with* you but IN you in His invisible, unlimited presence.

Let me give you an example of what Jesus means by saying, "I will send you another comforter." Suppose you have a dollar and I say, "Give me your dollar." You give me the dollar then I say, "Here is *another* dollar. This dollar is exactly like the dollar you gave me. It has the same purchasing power. You were willing to give me your dollar and I gave you another dollar, so you've lost nothing."

That's what Jesus is saying to His disciples:

"You think that if I go away you'll be orphans— you'll be left alone. But I will not leave you comfortless. I will not leave you orphans. I will send you another Comforter. I will send you the Holy Spirit who is *with* you now but He shall be *IN* you."

This was the turning point of all history. The Holy Spirit who was *with* these believers was now going to be IN them. Jesus Christ in the flesh was filled with the Holy Spirit. The Holy Spirit was working with these people who had faith in that day, but now Jesus is saying, "I'll go away but I'll send Him and He shall be IN you." This is another way of saying that God will come back through Jesus by the power of the Holy Spirit.

Jesus was saying:

"I will return but this time I'll be in My unlimited
form. I'll not be physical or visible. You won't see
Me with the eyes in your head. You won't hear
Me with the ears of your head. You won't touch
Me with the hands of your body. But you will see
Me with the eyes of your soul. You will hear Me
with the hearing of your spirit. You will feel Me
by the ability of your spirit to experience God. I'll
be IN you. You won't have to travel from Capernaum to Cana to get Me to come and heal your
little child. You won't have to go to Tulsa or New
York or Paris or London or the ends of the earth.
No, you won't have to go anywhere because the
Holy Spirit will be IN you. The kingdom of God
will come into you and you will not say, 'Lo, Christ
is here' or 'Christ is there' because the kingdom of
God will be WITHIN you."

As you have Christ living inside you by the power of
the Holy Spirit—you have **the whole explosive kingdom of
God inside you.** You are in position for the *works of the
Father* to be done in you and you don't have to go anywhere. Right where you stand, sit, or lie, the kingdom of
God is within you. Whether you are on a hospital bed . . .
in a classroom . . . in a machine shop . . . a law building . . .
a business establishment . . . working in the fields or in a
kitchen or in a pulpit, or anywhere else, Jesus Christ comes
to you through the power of the Holy Spirit. If you really
have Him, He is IN you and there is no distance.

THERE IS NO DISTANCE BETWEEN HIM AND YOU— THEREFORE THERE IS NO DISTANCE IN PRAYER

The first understanding I had of this great truth was
in the '50s. I received a letter from a woman in Baltimore,

Maryland. At the time, I was conducting a crusade in Oakland, California, so the letter went from the East Coast to the West Coast. It read like this:

Dear Brother Roberts:

I am very ill. I wanted to come to your Oakland Crusade and have you lay your hands upon me and pray for me but I do not have the money to travel. So I am writing you this letter instead and asking you to pray for me. **I realize there is no distance in prayer . . .**

A shock of comprehension swept through my being. It was an electrifying current of understanding. There I was some 2,000 or more miles from this woman and she believed in me and she believed in my prayers. But suddenly she transcended me. She went above and beyond me. She was no longer limited by me. She caught hold of a tremendous truth . . . THERE IS NO DISTANCE IN PRAYER. She went on to say:

You pray there, and I'll pray here and God will heal me. . .

Well, I prayed for her and wrote her back. In a short time I received another letter back from her, praising God for her healing.

This glorious truth came home to me again in a crusade in North Carolina. This was one of the largest crusades we had ever had. It imposed burdens upon me and upon the people because so many wanted to come through the prayer line at the same time and have me lay my hands upon them and pray. The larger the crowd grew, the more impossible it became for one man to do this. The crowds grew to 30,000 people in one day.

One night a young girl, 12 or 13 years old, was in the audience. She had been born with crooked legs. I mean, they were so bowed she wore her dresses nearly to her ankles because she was embarrassed for people to see the shape of her legs. Many times the children at school would laugh at her. Her mother and father had been born with misshapen limbs and evidently this condition was passed on to her. That night she was sitting in the back. I didn't know she was there. I didn't know she existed.

In that service I shared the letter from the woman in Baltimore who said, "There is no distance in prayer." From time to time I would ask the entire audience to stand and touch each other or hold the back of their chair as a *point of contact*. Then I'd stand there and pray that the Lord would heal. I would try to see Jesus' hands touching them where they were.

As the audience was getting ready to do as I said, this little girl was understanding something. She was saying in herself, "I wish I could go up into the healing line. I wish I could go there and have Brother Roberts pray for me. I believe I would be healed, but if I go for prayer people will see my legs." (I learned this later from her and her parents.)

Then she heard me say, "Why don't you just stand where you are and let me pray for you, for there is no distance in prayer." As the crowd stood up, she stood up. And as she stood up she said a warmth came into her legs and she felt something happening to them. She lifted her dress to her knees and she saw that her legs were perfectly straight. She grabbed her father and mother and said, "Look at my legs." The father found their pastor and told him. He immediately rushed to the platform and said, "Brother Roberts, let me bring a little girl from my church to the platform. A miracle has happened."

He brought her up and she stood there, no longer ashamed, and lifted that long dress to her knees and showed us how straight her legs were. I stood there so moved I was crying like a baby. I had not touched her. I'd not even prayed for her as an individual. She was just there in that crowd doing business with the King of kings and Lord of lords. I patted her hand and talked to her. I tried to get her to explain it to me but all she could say was, "You said Jesus could do it anywhere and He did."

That's about the best answer anybody can give. You can try to explain a miracle all you want to, but God either did it or He didn't. You either have a miracle or you don't. The more you try to explain a miracle, the harder it is. When it happens it really is simple—it is the *work of the Father*.

3. THE MIRACLE OF THE HEALING OF THE NOBLEMAN'S SON SAYS THAT YOUR BELIEVING IS KNOWING . . . YOUR FAITH IS KNOWING

There was a KNOWING in the heart of the nobleman. The Bible says he *believed* the words of Jesus Christ and went his way. His trip back home was interrupted by his people who came to meet him. They told him his child was healed. He asked, "When?" and they told him. And he KNEW that it was about the same hour that Jesus had said to him, "Go thy way; thy son liveth." Then his believing became even stronger. Now the substance of this really means . . . BELIEVING IS KNOWING. FAITH IS KNOWING. One of the best explanations of faith is:

> FAITH IS WHEN YOU REACH A POINT YOU CAN NO LONGER DOUBT . . . FAITH IS KNOWING!

Faith is not trying to make yourself believe, it is when you can no longer doubt. It's not trying to pump yourself up, or trying to force faith into yourself. Faith is reaching a point that no matter what you feel or don't feel in your

THE MIRACLES OF CHRIST

five senses, YOU KNOW! You know from deep within yourself, in your spirit, God is going to do it. Whether people
try to encourage or discourage you, *you know. That* is faith.

I realize there are many people who have difficulty serving the Lord. They have to have an awful lot of propping
up and encouragement. They have to be in the right spot
at the right time or they'll give up—or their friends believe
they will give up. This is because they really haven't gotten
through to what faith is.

There are others who are in desperate circumstances,
who are criticized and bullied and struck at, but you can't
shake their faith because they've reached a point of knowing. Had the nobleman not reached this place of knowing,
he would have been terribly upset there in Cana, frantic
with worry, wondering why Jesus wouldn't go to his house
. . . wondering why Jesus turned him down. But now the
nobleman KNOWS. He has reached the point where his
believing, his faith, has become a knowing. As I often say:

"I KNOW THAT I KNOW, THAT I KNOW,
THAT I KNOW."

How do I know? I just know that I know, that I know, that
I know.

In this miracle we again see the *three miracle keys of
Seed-Faith* at work. First, we see the nobleman looking to
Christ as the Source for the healing for his child (Key #1:
God is our Source—Philippians 4:19). Second, we see the
father investing his time, his concern, making the trip. Prob-
ably he did not realize at the time it was a seed of faith
that he was sowing (Key #2: Seeding for your miracle—
Luke 6:38).

Some people ask, "How can I go to a doctor and receive
help if I'm expecting God to be my Source?" In the first

place, you'll find the doctor's medicine works better if you really believe God is the Source of all healing. I believe your doctor will be more successful; several have personally told me this.

One doctor, who is a close friend of mine, developed a disease. He said to me, "I am being treated by doctors but I need your help." He had me to say again and again some of my phrases about God being the Source. Then he said, "If I can really believe God is my Source, somehow I believe this medicine will take effect."

And it's true. I believe everything works better if we know God is our Source and if we are planting seed—if we are giving something of ourselves—and if we are expecting a miracle.

Third, the nobleman went home expecting, didn't he? He went home *expecting*. He KNEW when he arrived home that little child would come running to meet him—restored once again to health (Key #3: Expect a miracle—Mark 11:24).

The campus of Oral Roberts University in Tulsa, Oklahoma, is the only university with a Prayer Tower at its center. Many believe it is the most unusual building of its kind in the world. It is 200 feet high. There, our Prayer Group is on duty 24 hours a day, 7 days a week, taking phone calls from people all over America and the continents. The calls average something over 1,000 a day, or more than 30,000 calls a month. People call who believe there is no distance in prayer. They call and they share, telling what their problems and needs are. They pour out their hearts and a prayer partner prays for them. Then their name and need is given to me so I can also pray and believe for them.

You see . . .
> You don't have to pray hard, you can pray easy . . .
> Prayer doesn't heal, God does.
> And there is no distance in God's healing
> power.

IN SUMMARY, THE SECOND MIRACLE OF JESUS—
THE HEALING OF THE NOBLEMAN'S SON—SAYS TO
YOU IN THE NOW:

1. **Jesus Christ is person-centered. He cares about You!**
   God is always in the midst of life and you don't have
   to worry about interrupting Him—you can reach
   Him at *any* time . . . with *any* need you have. He is
   at the point of your need.
2. **There is no distance in faith,** no distance in prayer.
3. **Believing is knowing. Faith is knowing.** Faith is not
   trying to make yourself believe . . . it is a knowing
   deep down inside that cannot be shaken. Faith is
   being able to say, "I KNOW THAT I KNOW,
   THAT I KNOW, THAT I KNOW!"
4. **You can help bring healing to a loved one.** Jesus
   doesn't have to physically be there. You can pray
   where you are, Jesus can act upon it, and your
   loved one can experience it in himself—no matter
   the distance.

3

CHRIST'S MIRACLE
FOR YOUR ACHE AND PAIN
IN TODAY'S WORLD OF STRESS
AND PRESSURE

John 6:5-14 says:

> *When Jesus then lifted up his eyes, and saw a great company come unto him, he saith unto Philip, Whence shall we buy bread, that these may eat? And this he said to prove him: for he himself knew what he would do. Philip answered him, Two hundred pennyworth of bread is not sufficient for them, that every one of them may take a little.* (This miracle is also recorded in the other three Gospels—Matthew 14:13-21, Mark 6:32-44, and Luke 9:10-17. In each account Jesus commands the disciples to feed the people. Here in the Gospel of John, He said, "Whence shall we buy bread, that these may eat?" In the other three accounts, Jesus said, "Give ye them to eat.") *One of his disciples, Andrew, Simon Peter's brother, saith unto him, There is a lad here, which hath five barley loaves, and two small fishes: but what are they among so many? And Jesus said, Make the men sit down . . . in number about five thousand. And Jesus took the loaves; and when he had given thanks, he distributed to the disciples, and the disciples to them that were set down; and likewise of the fishes as much as*

they would. When they were filled, he said unto his disciples, Gather up the fragments that remain, that nothing be lost. Therefore they gathered them together, and filled twelve baskets with the fragments of the five barley loaves, which remained over and above unto them that had eaten. Then those men, when they had seen the miracle that Jesus did, said, This is of a truth that prophet that should come into the world.

EVERYBODY HAS A PROBLEM . . . or he is a problem . . . or he lives with one. People have problems today until their problems have problems. This is why the miracle of the feeding of five thousand has such a special meaning to you in the now. This is Jesus Christ entering into the BREAD needs of you, a human being in the NOW. This is Jesus being concerned about you and your problems. This is Jesus Christ saying:

"I'm concerned about you. You are important to me. I am touched by the feelings of your infirmities . . . your problems . . . your needs."

Can you imagine . . . can you conceive for a moment that God can be touched, that He can feel the tragic things you experience? Well, He can! This miracle says to you:

GOD IS A TOTAL GOD FOR THE TOTAL MAN . . . FOR THE SPIRIT, THE MIND AND THE BODY . . . FOR THE CIRCUMSTANCES, EVERYTHING THAT YOU EXPERIENCE — THE HEARTACHE, THE HEADACHE, THE TOEACHE, THE STOMACHACHE, THE POCKETBOOK ACHE, THE ECONOMIC ACHE, THE POLITICAL ACHE, THE RELIGIOUS ACHE, THE EXAMINATION ACHE, THE CHILDREN ACHE! GOD IS A TOTAL GOD FOR THE NOW OF YOUR ACHE!

This may sound humorous—that is, if you are not hurting. But this is an age when people do hurt. They hurt deep inside. They hurt because they can't pay their bills . . . they can't understand their children . . . they have a hard time of keeping their marriages from falling apart.

You hurt . . . you ache . . . and Jesus is *concerned!*

In this miracle we find a great crowd of people following Jesus into the desert. Eager to listen to Him preach, they lose all track of time and distance. Now they are in a desert and it's suppertime. But there are no stores, restaurants, or anything of that nature. In fact, they are so far from town that Jesus fears if He sends them away they will faint by the wayside . . . they won't make it.

This is an economic problem and a political one, too. It is quite similar to the economic and political failures in this, our own time. We see inflation rampant. Unemployment is high. Bills are piling up on every side. Prices are rising beyond comprehension. People are having a desperate time of actually getting something to eat . . . of being able to make the car payments . . . or pay the rent or make the house payments. For many dear people, things are falling completely apart. This has created a feeling of gloom and fear.

I, of necessity, have to be a business man as well as an evangelist and educator. Many times I attend business meetings. In those meetings they talk about how bad things are and when I leave I literally have to fight off the spirit of gloom and despair. You know what I mean. You hear many of the same things. You read it in the newspapers and hear it on television. After awhile you begin to wonder what you have to look forward to . . . if things are ever going to get better. And fear builds up inside you.

Well, our Lord looked out over that desperate crowd. The Bible says there were five thousand men *plus* women and children, so this means many thousands more. And Jesus sees their fear. He sees they are hungry. The children are beginning to whimper and the parents are wondering, how can we feed them here? Jesus looked but He saw more than just a mass of people . . . *He individualized each one of them as a person. Then He individualized each one's need.*

The fact is, Jesus Christ was very much in the tradition of doing His Father's works. That is, He was manifesting the love and concern of heaven toward people's lives wherever they were. The Lord's Prayer was actually going to be fulfilled. In this prayer Jesus taught us to pray:

> *Our Father which art in heaven, Hallowed be thy name. Thy kingdom come. Thy will be done in earth as it is in heaven. Give us this day our daily bread* . . . (Matthew 6:9-11).

There on that hillside that day Jesus was thinking of BREAD. He was thinking of the hunger in their stomachs. He individualized each one as a person, each one with a need. Jesus knew each one needed money to buy bread. And Jesus individualized the distance they would have to travel in order to buy bread—if they had the money, that is.

Jesus was there . . . with the multitude . . . with each individual person . . . He was there with them in their need. JESUS IS ALWAYS AT THE POINT OF YOUR NEED. If you want to know where Jesus is, that's where He is. He's at the point of your need. How difficult that is to remember when you've got an aching head, or a fever, or a sick child, or someone dear to you is sick, or you are facing a problem that's tearing you up. But it is true—wherever the need is, Jesus is standing right there and He's teaching you to say to the Father, "Give us this day our daily bread. Thy kingdom come, thy will be done to me on earth as it is in heaven." Jesus is saying . . .

HEAVEN AND EARTH SHOULD TOUCH
EACH OTHER IN YOUR LIFE

He's saying you should be able to taste of heaven now so you'll know what it is like when you get there. He's saying that earth is not so removed from heaven that they are dissimilar. Jesus says that earth and heaven belong together.

How in the world could you ever enjoy heaven if you don't enjoy the kingdom of heaven down here? If the kingdom of heaven doesn't touch you in the NOW, how is it going to touch you in eternity? If your religious experience is drab, empty, and meaningless now, how could heaven ever be meaningful to you? If you never get any bread now, how could you enjoy the bread of heaven? Jesus is saying:

"Give us this day—TODAY IN THE NOW—our daily bread. Thy will be done in earth—NOW—as it is in heaven."

We ought to start acting now like we are going to act when we get to heaven. I want you to know that God wants to open up the windows of heaven in the *now!*

God wants to help you with your problems and needs in the NOW!

IN THE MIRACLE OF THE FEEDING OF THE FIVE THOUSAND JESUS SHOWS US THAT THE WORKS OF THE FATHER ARE TO CONTINUE ... AND THEY ARE TO CONTINUE THROUGH YOU AND ME.

Jesus said to the disciples, "Give *ye* them to eat."

And they said, "Send them away. Let them buy for themselves."

Jesus said, "They need not depart, give *ye* them to eat."

There's a whole world of difference in philosophy between the twelve disciples and Jesus Christ. They said, "Yes, we know the people are hungry, send them away." But Jesus said, "No, they need not depart. You give them to eat." The disciples were saying, "The situation is too tough; there's nothing we can do." But Jesus was saying, "With God all things are possible!"

Then the disciples said, "We have so little, how can we feed them?"

Jesus is having a real problem here with the word *miracle*. In their minds the disciples are indicating *it's going to take a miracle*.

In Christ's own mind He is saying, "No, it's just another *work of the Father*. If I can just do the works of the Father through your cooperation, I can teach you how to continue doing these works of the Father. Then you can help people get their needs met and in getting theirs met, you are going to get yours met."

Here we have the clear teaching of the miracle of Seed-Faith. We have Jesus indicating He has a plan. The Bible says, *For he himself knew what He would do.*

JESUS HAD A PLAN—A PLAN OF SEED-FAITH

Jesus had a plan of action through which He would do His Father's works . . . through which He would feed the five thousand. That plan began with an act on the part of His followers. He said, "Give *ye* them to eat."

They said, "But we have so little."

He said, "Then take of that little you have and give."

Notice in Matthew 17:20, Jesus said:

> *If ye have faith as a grain of mustard seed, ye shall say unto this mountain, Remove hence to yonder place; and it shall remove; and nothing shall be impossible unto you.*

Here Jesus talks about the smallest of seeds . . . the mustard seed. He says:

> "You can have faith in a very small way. But if you can have just a little bit of faith and release that faith then you can say to your mountain of need, 'Be removed.' And it shall remove! Don't start with trying to move the mountain, start with putting in the seed . . . the seed of faith."

Jesus is saying, "You put the seed in first before you start on your problem."

In contrast, we begin by wrestling with the problem, sometimes we wrestle with it until it gets us down. But Jesus says, **"Start giving, start putting the seed in** and then the seed will release the power of God to move the mountain" (the problem).

Jesus said, "Give ye them to eat." The whole plan Jesus had started with their giving—and giving first.

Finally Andrew, one of the disciples who had led his brother Simon Peter to Christ, said, "There is a lad here, which hath five barley loaves and two small fishes: but what are they among so many?"

That is a good question, but the important thing is that Andrew is now performing an act of giving. He has located a little boy who apparently is the only one with any food. Andrew brings him to Christ and he gives Jesus something to work with. *Here is seed for a miracle.*

SEEDING FOR ONE'S OWN MIRACLE IS THE MOST IMPORTANT THING

At this point many Christians, whether they admit it or not, become very displeased with God. The miracle they need doesn't come so they begin to accuse God. They wander away from God. They openly accuse God or they secretly harbor resentment against Him. But they have not put the seed in. They've not started the way God starts. They've not learned how God works. They've not listened. They've not learned. And I certainly am among that number from time to time. But it's not God's fault. We've not put the seed in, and if we don't, God has nothing to work with.

Think a minute about the death of our Lord. This was the greatest seed of all time. The seed of faith that stands supreme is our Lord giving himself on the cross. The greatest miracle . . . or the greatest resurrection . . . or the greatest harvest of all time . . . is His rising from the dead. But the seed of His resurrection was planted by himself first by giving His life on the cross. Jesus put the seed in *first* . . .the seed of His own life. That seed was the one from which God raised Him from the dead. So we have here in the death and resurrection of Christ, sowing and reaping, seed-time and harvest, which means we have the miracle of Seed-Faith.

Death represents the enemy. It represents what the devil does to you, which is bad. It represents what he takes from you, how he diminishes you, how he depletes your resources, how he reduces you in your circumstances, how he discourages and distresses you, how he gets you with your back to the wall, how he makes you feel you are going to fail so that you say, "I'm not going to make it." You see, the devil is trying to destroy you.

Now when you begin giving of your inner self, giving of your love, your concern, your compassion, your money, you are putting a seed in. You are giving our Lord something to work a miracle with. In that giving, a part of you is dying —a part of you is being given up just as Jesus gave up His life on the cross. That giving is a seed and that seed is what God uses to resurrect, to bring back to you what you gave Him, to multiply it back.

In the parable of the sower Jesus told how the multiplication of the seed was either thirtyfold or sixtyfold or a hundredfold (Mark 4:1-20). That's some great return, isn't it?

JESUS PROMISES YOU THAT EVERY SEED YOU PLANT WILL COME BACK AGAIN ... AND AGAIN ... AND AGAIN ... BIGGER ... AND BIGGER ... AND BIGGER. THE SEED YOU PLANT WILL EXPLODE INTO THE MEETING OF YOUR TOTAL NEED. HE SAYS TO YOU: GOD'S WHOLE UNIVERSE OF RESOURCES ARE AVAILABLE TO YOU!

In this age when prices are going up and inflation is everywhere, people are gloomy and they don't know what to do. Jesus says you are not to operate by man-made laws alone. He says that you, as His child, are to operate by a higher law—which is the eternal law of God. Jesus is dealing here with an actual condition of hunger and economic difficulty. He's dealing with people's gloom and doubt and inability to handle their problems. He's dealing with a really bad human situation and He's saying, "Give Me something to work with."

Finally Andrew brought the little lad with his lunch of five loaves and two fishes to Jesus.

In slow motion we see how Jesus multiplies this seed of faith. I can see the little boy sitting or standing, hugging his lunch to him, or holding it in his hand, when a man approaches him, whose name is Andrew. He says, "The Master would like to have your lunch. Would you give it to Jesus?"

"Yes," the little boy says, "If Jesus has sent word that that's what He needs . . . something to work a miracle with . . . I'll give it to Him!"

The little boy has no difficulty believing that God can do anything, that God can make a way where there is no way.

The older we get, the more we let the devil cheat us and the harder it is for us to believe as a little child believes. A little child is so fresh out of heaven; his faith is fresh. I mean, he's seen God since we have.

I think perhaps Jesus said to the lad, "Son, do you believe I could feed these people, thousands of them, with your lunch?"

"Sure, Jesus, You can do it. You can do it, Jesus."

Do you see the boy finding his Source? Do you see him looking at Jesus as the Source of his total supply. Do you see him willingly giving his lunch? There's no indication the little boy resented it, or rejected it, or said, "I'm scared to give it to You," or, "If I give it to You, I'll be diminished. I'll lose out. I'll never get it back." The little boy is practicing Seed-Faith. He is saying, "God is my Source. I'll put my seed in. Sure, I'll expect a miracle. Jesus, You can do anything."

Jesus is trying to get us to be like little children rather than folks who think they are so smart they have the answer to all the problems. Of course, when the problems get big enough we have to admit that even we can't cut it. The nation gets upset, business gets upset, and God is saying to us, "Just hold steady. I have an eternal law that goes all the way back to Genesis 8:22:"

> *While the earth remaineth, seedtime and harvest . . . shall not cease.*

God is saying, "Put the seed in, you'll reap what you sow" (Galatians 6:7). He's saying, "He who gives seed to the sower will multiply the seed sown" (2 Corinthians 9:10). He's saying, "Give, and it shall be given unto you" (Luke 6:38). He's saying, "Give Me this little lunch and I'll feed this entire crowd."

As I said, in slow motion, we see Jesus as He takes the lunch—five barley loaves and two small fishes. The Bible says, first, He gave thanks for it. Second, the Bible says, He broke it.

THE SCIENCE OF THE SITUATION

A scientific question emerges, "Is Jesus releasing the atoms that are in the bread?" It's a very serious question. How is Jesus doing this? They say that in one little pound of coal there is enough heat stored up to heat an entire city, if we could learn how to release the atoms in it. Our scientists discovered how to split the atom and to cause a chain reaction. Then they created a monster bomb that leveled two cities in Japan. Today there are thousands and thousands of these bombs held by America, Russia, France, England, China, India, and possibly other nations. We are scared to death. We are frightened of these unholy instruments of death.

On the other hand, the scientists are saying that the same atom power which can be released for evil can be released for good. Is Jesus now releasing the atoms in a few pieces of bread and a few pieces of fish? Is this a miracle, or is it another work of the Father? Is Jesus just simply doing what He knows to do with what He created?

Jesus gave thanks. Then He broke the bread. He handed it to His disciples and as he handed it out it never diminished. Every time He gave a handful, there was another handful for a disciple to take and to hand out.

Was this a release of atoms? Was it a scientific breakthrough? Is it time for our scientists to catch up with God's own miracle-working power? Do we have to face the threat of a hungry world and worry ourselves to death about overpopulation? Not if we believe in God . . . not if we have faith. The population may become so huge it's uncountable but if we become like a little child and have faith in God, there will be a way for every man to eat. There are so many without jobs that it seems like there will never be enough, but the man who practices Seed-Faith and the woman who practices Seed-Faith operates on a higher level. And he or she will be taken care of. I believe that, I know that.

I believe it because I cannot exist even 30 more days without it. I cannot operate Oral Roberts University and our television ministry. All the things we do require an annual budget of millions of dollars, not a dime of which I have. We have buildings going up and more buildings are needed at ORU. We have students with needs, partners all over the world with needs. We receive thousands of letters every month, over half of which are from people who are desperate, who have terrible needs. Some of them are without food. They are without jobs. Their bills are piling up. Others have committed sins that are tearing them apart. Many write whose homes are breaking up, their marriages are falling apart. But I tell you that . . .

THE WORKS OF GOD ARE NOT OVER. JESUS CHRIST IS THE SAME YESTERDAY, TODAY, AND FOREVER. IF YOU'LL HAVE FAITH AS A SEED AND PLANT IT, GOD WILL MULTIPLY IT. GOD WILL DO A WORK IN YOUR LIFE THAT WILL SOLVE YOUR PROBLEM!

I'd rather be like that little boy with two little fish and five loaves, and have my faith in God my Source, than to be the richest man in the world and be scared to death that someone's going to kill me, or scared I was going to run out of money, or scared of the economy. I'd rather be like that little boy and hand my little seed to Jesus and say, "Jesus, You can do it. You can take care of me. You can take care of all my needs."

When the crowd had been filled—the Bible says, "Every man was filled"—Jesus said, "Gather up what's left."

They gathered up 12 basketsful! They started with a handful. They fed five thousand men plus many more women and children. And then they gathered up 12 basketsful of leftovers!

I believe Jesus gave the 12 basketsful to the little boy. The Bible doesn't say He did, but the Bible doesn't say that He didn't either. So there is as much Scripture for it as against it!

TWO MEN

A rich man and a poor man were walking side by side. The rich man was so tight and stingy he wouldn't give anybody anything so he lost all his friends but one. This poor man and he were walking down the road when it began to rain. As they crossed a bridge the poor man slipped and fell into the lake. He couldn't swim and his first thought was to cry out to his rich friend, "Give me your hand." Then it dawned upon him that this man wouldn't give anyone *anything*, so quickly he said, "Here, take my hand. *Take* mine."

The rich man *took* his hand and pulled him out.

Christianity's way is not: "Give me this" or "Give me that." Christianity's way is: "I'll give. I'll love. I'll go out of my way. I'll go the second mile. I'll help you. I'll pick you up. I'll smile. I'll assist you." And we do it joyfully.

In Matthew 25:35-40, we read some of the most remarkable words our Lord ever said:

> For I was an hungred, and ye gave me meat: I was thirsty, and ye gave me drink: I was a stranger, and ye took me in: Naked, and ye clothed me: I was sick, and ye visited me: I was in prison, and ye came unto me. Then shall the righteous answer him, saying, Lord, when saw we thee an hungred, and fed thee? or thirsty, and gave thee drink? When saw we thee a stranger, and took thee in? or naked, and clothed thee? Or when saw we thee sick, or in prison, and came unto thee? And the King shall answer and say unto them, Verily I say unto you, Inasmuch as ye have done it unto one of the least . . . ye have done it unto me.

This means whenever you and I give or put in our seed we are doing it unto Jesus. **The person we feed becomes Jesus to us.** The person we visit in prison or in the sickbed becomes Jesus to us. How may we know our Lord? We know Him in doing His works. We know Him in putting our arms around those who are desperate, because when we do that we are putting our arms around Jesus Christ. We are not saying, "Here, give me your hand." We are saying, "Here, take mine." It is God's way of discipleship that never fails. It will never let you down, nor me.

As I face my problems (which I think are enormous, just as you think your problems are overwhelming) I talk to myself and I say, "Oral Roberts, quit trying to *get* and start learning to *give*. Put in a seed. Give our Lord something to work with. Help somebody and you are helping Jesus. Then

Jesus is going to give thanks and break it and hand it out, and you will be filled. Your own needs will be met."

SUMMARY

WHENEVER YOU READ ABOUT THE MIRACLE OF THE FEEDING OF THE FIVE THOUSAND I WANT YOU TO REMEMBER THIS:

1. **Jesus is concerned about your "bread" needs.**

   He wants to give you your daily bread . . . to meet your needs—financial, physical, spiritual— whatever that need may be.

2. **Heaven and earth should touch each other in your life.**

   God wants you to enjoy the riches of heaven now . . . He wants to give *you* bread—TODAY . . . IN THE NOW OF YOUR NEED.

3. **Seeding for your miracle is the most important thing you can do.**

   When you have a need that is like a mountain before you, forget about the need and start giving. Start planting the seed. Then the seed of faith will release the power of God to move the mountain (need).

4. **The seed you give will be multiplied back to you . . . again and again and again . . . bigger and bigger and bigger (Mark 4:1-20). So expect your miracle.**

5. **The works of God are not over. Jesus Christ is the same yesterday, today, and forever (Hebrews 13:8).**

   If you will have faith as a seed and plant it, God will multiply it. God will be there to do a work in your life that will solve your problem! But again, you must expect it.

4

CHRIST'S DAILY MIRACLE
FOR ALL YOUR FINANCIAL NEEDS

*And it came to pass, that, as the people pressed upon
him (our Lord) to hear the word of God, he stood by
the lake of Gennesaret (sea of Galilee), And saw two
ships standing by the lake, but the fishermen were gone
out of them, and were washing their nets. And he
(Jesus) entered into one of the ships, which was Simon's, and prayed him that he would thrust out a little
from the land. And he sat down, and taught the people
out of the ship. Now when he had left speaking, he said
unto Simon, Launch out into the deep, and let down
your nets for a draught (catch). And Simon answering
said unto him, Master, we have toiled all the night, and
have taken nothing: nevertheless at thy word I will let
down the net. And when they had this done, they in-
closed a great multitude of fishes: and their net brake.
And they beckoned unto their partners, which were in
the other ship, that they should come and help them.
And they came, and filled both the ships, so that they
began to sink. When Simon Peter saw it, he fell down at
Jesus' knees, saying, Depart from me; for I am a sinful
man, O Lord. For he was astonished, and all that were
with him, at the draught (catch) of the fishes which they*

had taken: And so was also James, and John, the sons of Zebedee, which were partners with Simon. And Jesus said unto Simon, Fear not; from henceforth thou shall catch men. And when they had brought their ships to land they forsook all, and followed him (Luke 5:1-11).

IF I HAVE A FAVORITE MIRACLE of Jesus, it is THE MIRACLE CATCH OF FISH. This miracle is a real picture of our lives. I'd like to ask you a very personal question. Are you facing some kind of futility? Is there a problem in your life that defies you at every turn and seemingly will not turn loose? Do you have a need that baffles you, that boggles your mind? Is there something that has held on so long until your past is more dominant than your present . . . and your past is having a negative effect upon your future? Then this miracle has a tremendous meaning for you.

These fishermen here in Luke 5 were washing and mending their nets. They were businessmen. They plied the sea with their ships, catching fish and selling them commercially as far away as Jerusalem. This was the way they made their living. So when they failed to catch fish, it would be like a businessman failing to make sales, or a farmer failing to have a harvest, or a father or mother failing with their family, or a marriage falling apart, or something not working in a person's life. It meant futility and frustration. They were sitting there by their empty boats, having been out upon the sea, and failed completely. They may have been thinking, *the sea apparently is not going to be productive during this season. It's going to be a bad season. It's going to be a bad time. The economy is going to break down. Inflation will take over. There will be problems upon problems and needs piled upon needs. Even our problems will have problems.*

About this time something *good happened!* And I
believe . . .

SOMETHING GOOD IS GOING TO HAPPEN TO YOU

I don't think we're any different than the people were
back there. We have our problems too. I've never met anyone who didn't have a problem. I have them and you have
them. It's a lot like the physician who was talking to me
recently. He said, "Can I ever get *all* my problems solved?"

I said, "When you get one problem solved, there will be
another one to take its place."

He said, "Oh, no!"

I said, "Oh, yes! That's just the way life is. Life is a
problem-solving process. There will always be problems until
the day we die. And if we're not right with God we'll have a
greater problem at death than we've had in life. So our only
hope is to find a Source . . . a Source for our lives . . . a Source
for our supply. We are going to have to learn who our Source
is. We are going to have to learn that this Source—who is
God—has His way of doing things, and to learn how to do
things His way so that we will be in the process of problem-
solving rather than the process of problems riding us down
all the time and keeping us beaten down."

This miracle of Jesus is a NOW miracle. At this deepest
moment of discouragement in the lives of these commercial
fishermen, Jesus Christ walks up. Now that says a lot. JESUS
CHRIST IS WHERE THE NEED IS. I believe the Bible
teaches us to look for Him where the need is. We are to look
for Him at the point of a need that we have or the problem
that we are facing. I realize, personally, this is not easy. It's
easier to think of the problem than it is to think about the
Lord. It's easier to dwell upon the need than upon anything
else.

I dealt with a young man recently. He had had an operation on his shoulder. He also had a very bad experience in his marriage. In fact, his past experience was so bad he couldn't think of anything else. As we prayed he would feel better—for a time. Then we'd start to talk again and immediately he would slip back into the past. Finally I said to him, "If we don't give this past to God, it's going to destroy you."

He said, "Well, what shall I do with my past?"

I said, "**The only thing you can do with your past is to give it to God because you cannot relive it.** God cannot place into your hands the opportunities of yesterday. They are gone. All you can do with your past—or I can do with my past—is to give it to God. Let God have it. Otherwise, it's going to direct your life backward all the time."

CHRIST CAME UPON THIS SCENE BY THE SEA OF GALILEE TO REDIRECT PETER'S THOUGHTS AND THE THOUGHTS OF THESE FISHERMEN FROM THE PAST OF FUTILITY AND FAILURE TO THE PRESENT OF DELIVERANCE AND SUCCESS.

I firmly believe **God wants you to be successful.** God is not interested in anyone being a failure. The Bible says:

Beloved, I wish above all things that thou mayest PROSPER and be in health, even as thy soul prospereth (3 John 2).

This is God's wish for you. If God had His way all the time, things would be different in the world. Things would be better in your life and in my life. Therefore, I say again, we need to learn who our Source is and how this Source, who is God, does things. God has a way of doing things. I call it the miracle of Seed-Faith. If you make Seed-Faith a way of life you are going to get a lot more of your problems solved.

You are going to get into a rhythm of success. You'll find things falling into place. You'll be getting yourself together better. You'll be finding yourself coming into a wholeness in a more direct way than you have in the past.

Now Jesus Christ walks up and He is followed by a tremendous crowd. They want to hear Him preach. They want to receive His blessing. He stands there on the seashore ready to preach but He has no place to stand where He can be seen. He looks around and He sees some fishermen sitting there in the sand with their fishing nets in their hands. Obviously they have not become aware of Jesus. These old nets are wearing out. Over here is their big boat. It's empty. It's turned over on the side. On the faces of the fishermen are the signs of the struggle of the previous night. They've been out on the water to catch fish which meant money for their families.

The fishermen always fish at night on the sea of Galilee and never during the day because the waters are sparkling clear. I've seen those waters. I've been upon them many times and I can understand why they fished at night and not during the day. The water is so clear the fish would see the net if it's thrown into the water during the day, so they have to fish in the dark of the moon where the fish cannot see the net. So these men had been out there when all the signs were right. They had fished in the normal way. They had done everything in the way they were supposed to do them to get their lives together, to get their needs met. They had kept all the rules of the economy. They had done it right, according to man, and now they are sitting there with failure and futility.

I believe they felt lonely and deserted. Perhaps they said, "Why has this happened to us? What have we done to deserve it?" I feel that way at times and you feel that way at times. What about the feeling of Jesus Christ? I see *two concerns* that our Lord had:

1. Jesus was very concerned about the *spiritual* needs of that great audience and He wanted to preach to them, to offer them the good news of the gospel.

2. I see Jesus' second concern is a concern for the *secular*, or material needs. Jesus saw those fishermen with their broken nets and empty boats, their discouraged hearts, their empty wallets, and the futility of a tomorrow. A serious material problem is facing them and Jesus Christ becomes deeply concerned about it.

I see something else—I see *two needs:*

1. **Jesus Christ has a need.** He has a need for the great work of God to be done. He needed a pulpit. He knows the empty boat would be perfect, especially if it were pushed a little from the shore. Then he could stand in it and the people could gather around the edge of the sea and it would just be a beautiful preaching situation. Our Lord needed their boat.

2. **The fishermen needed a miracle.** They needed a redirection of their thoughts. They needed to discover a Source for their lives. They needed to know who is behind the natural laws. They also needed to know that there are higher laws—there are eternal laws through which they could get their needs met when everything else failed.

I see those two needs. Then I see something else. I see Jesus saying to the fishermen, "Lend Me your boat. Give Me your boat. GIVE ME A SEED TO MATCH YOUR NEED." Please notice that Jesus asks them to give out of their need. Here they are desperately in need and He is asking for the very instrument through which they make their living. He's asking for it and they give to Him . . . out of their need. So they loaned Him their empty boat.

I see that when they loan their boat to Jesus, it is empty. But when He returns the boat, it is full. I see that Jesus Christ has an entirely different outlook on us than we do of each other. When Jesus asks you for something, He wants you to get into an attitude of loving and giving. He has a purpose in mind for you. He is concerned about the need you are facing. He wants to meet that need. Here He asks for an empty boat with the very great purpose of using it for His own service and then returning it with overflowing success. You see . . .

GOD IS A GOOD GOD AND THE DEVIL IS A BAD DEVIL.

GOD IS TOTALLY GOOD AND THE DEVIL IS TO- TALLY BAD.

THERE'S NO BADNESS IN GOD AND THERE'S NO GOODNESS IN THE DEVIL.

OUR GOD IS A GOOD GOD.

The fishermen loaned Jesus their boat and He used it to speak the gospel from. There He stands. Can you see Him out there in the boat preaching, speaking the words of life to the individuals in that great audience? All of a sudden He stops and He speaks to these fishermen who have loaned Him their boat. They are sitting there in the boat as He preaches and He speaks to them. Before, it appeared He only wanted something from them but now we see what it's all about. He says, "Launch out into the deep and let down your net for a catch."

In other words, Jesus was saying, "I realize this boat is empty. I'm aware your nets are worn. I see the futility of your existence and I'm going to do something about it.

You've loaned Me your boat. You've given Me a seed to match your need. You've given me something to work with. Now launch out into the deep and let down your nets for a catch."

And Peter cried right back, "O Lord, we've toiled all night and taken nothing."

It was a natural reaction. When God speaks to you to start giving of what you have, to start taking something and making a seed of faith of it and putting it into His hands, it is very difficult for you to understand. In Matthew 17:20, Jesus said:

> *If ye have faith as a grain of mustard seed, ye shall say unto this mountain* (this mountain of need), *Remove hence to yonder place; and it shall remove; and nothing shall be impossible unto you.*

Jesus Christ talks a lot about seed. He talks a lot about giving. He talks about giving in such a way that He says it is more blessed (more productive) to give than to receive (Acts 20:35). He tells you that only what you give is multiplied back . . . not what you receive. What you *give* is multiplied back. In other words, what you seed with, what you put into the ground as a seed—like the farmer— is multiplied back in the harvest. Not that which is taken *from* the harvest, but that which is put into the ground, or planted, is multiplied back.

IT'S NOT WHAT YOU RECEIVE THAT IS MULTIPLIED— IT IS WHAT YOU GIVE THAT IS MULTIPLIED

This is what Jesus is teaching here. He shows His concern; He shows His response when people give to Him. You can count on that response. He never changes. Jesus said in Luke 6:38:

Give, and it shall be given unto you.

Here Jesus is talking about giving in the deepest sense of the word . . . the giving of yourself. How do you give yourself? You give in different ways. You give of your love . . . you give of your money . . . you give of your time . . . you give of your talent . . . you give of your concern. You are in a continual state of giving of yourself. You make up your mind that this is the nature of God: God is a God of love; God is a God of giving; God is always giving and loving and responding to you. And God is saying, "Be like Jesus . . . give . . . love . . . respond with your entire being . . . and make of it a seed and that seed will be multiplied back."

In other words, Jesus said, "You have loaned Me your boat. I've used it. Now I see your need and I'm going to multiply what you've given *back* to you. You gave Me an empty boat. But when I give it back to you this boat is going to be filled."

There was no way for these fishermen to comprehend what Jesus was saying because it's now broad daylight and it's unnatural in the sea of Galilee to try to fish during the day. But Jesus is saying, "Break the rules! Break the rules! *Break the rules that are set by man that circumscribe God. Break the rules that say God is not concerned about your needs.*"

Man says, "Where is God? Why does God allow war to break out? Why does God allow inflation to become so great? Why does God allow so much unemployment? Why does God allow this sickness to strike me? Why does God do this?" Man asks this about God. As a result, man thinks: *God is not concerned; He's not interested; God is not involved in our human affairs and because of that, as human*

*beings we are going to make our own rules to regulate our
economy. We are going to make our own rules as to how we
recover from our sicknesses. We are going to make our own
rules as to how we solve our marriage problems or how we
can solve our relationships with other people.* So we have
made a set of man-made rules which are indicated here by
these men who were saying, "The fishing rules are that you
do it this way."

And Jesus says, "No, while that is a good way to fish, it
is not the *only* way to fish. I can show you there is a greater
way to fish, because now I want to multiply the seed sown.
I want to give back to you as you have given to God."

Peter said, "Lord, we've toiled all night and taken nothing. There's no way that we can find any fish."

I'd like to say this:

GOD CAN MAKE THINGS DO WHAT THEY DON'T
ORDINARILY DO.

GOD CAN MAKE THINGS HAPPEN THAT THE
    RULES SAY CANNOT HAPPEN.

GOD CAN MAKE A WAY FOR YOU WHERE
    THERE IS NO WAY.

When you give Him a seed of faith, or you start giving
of yourself and you give Him something to work with, then
you are breaking the rules that man has set. If you live
within these man-made laws completely, then when unemployment comes you say, "There aren't enough jobs to go
around." I believe Jesus teaches that if you keep your seeds
of faith flowing into God, and you start having unemployment problems, God will take care of you. God will take care
of your problem. You can change the effect of this society
upon you because you operate by a higher law, a law that's
older and that is God's eternal law—the law of sowing and
reaping.

"We've toiled all night," Simon Peter said, "and taken nothing. Nevertheless, at thy word, Jesus, I will let down the net." Here Peter is beginning to switch, to redirect his thinking. He's beginning to discover a Source for his life. He doesn't know it right now. He's only thinking about this fishing trip, that maybe there's a possibility of success if he'll launch out and do what Christ says.

A little later we are going to see that Peter's involvement with Christ goes much deeper than this. It starts out as a surface one. It begins with the need he has. People say, "Well, you only want God for a fire escape." Well, that's partly right. I certainly would like to get out of the fire. Some say, "You only want God for the loaves and fishes." That's true, I want to be fed. Others say, "You only want God when you have a need." Yes, sir, He's the best One for me to want when I have a need. You see, I admit a lot of these things, but I also go beyond that. I believe . . .

TRUE SEED-FAITH BEGINS WITH THE NEED YOU HAVE BUT IT BRINGS YOU INTO AN INVOLVEMENT AND PARTICIPATION WITH JESUS CHRIST UNTIL YOU TRULY FOLLOW HIM AND BECOME HIS DISCIPLE.

It may begin with a physical need or a financial need or a need that is secular, but it ends up as a total need of your being, with God supplying all your needs—spiritual and financial and physical and material. It becomes a way of life. You make God your Source . . . you give . . . and you expect a miracle! Then God comes in and shows you how to solve the problem.

Peter said, "Nevertheless, at thy word I will let down the net. I will do it because You said to." Peter is indicating, "I don't understand it. I don't comprehend how we can get this done. I don't see any chance of our having success because You are requiring us to throw our nets over during the day when we can only do it successfully at night. We were unsuccessful in doing it last night but we are going to do it Your way now because You said to."

This is faith. This is when you come to a point where you accept what God says. You come to a point where you say, **"God, I'm going to give You my best then I'm going to ask You for Your best."** You say, "God, I don't understand how You will do it but I believe You will. God, Your way is not my way but I'm going to submit my way to Your way. I'm going to take the Bible and believe it. The world says the Bible is just another piece of great literature and that it is not the Word of God, but I am going to believe it is the Word of God. I'm going to try to follow the teachings of the Bible."

In our language today Peter is saying, "I've tried it on my own. I've failed. Now I'll do it Your way, God. I'll do it because You said to. I'll do it because of Your Word."

You see, this is turning to God and making Him the Source. Notice that Peter has made the sea of Galilee his source but now he is turning to the Lord as his Source. It's a complete reversal of his thinking.

There's a difference between an *instrument* and a *source*. A source is where it all comes from. An instrument could be anything that is useful at a given time. If the instrument fails after you've placed all your faith in it, then you are really in bad shape. But if you always go to the Source, the Source never runs out.

For example, an orchard: If you make the apples on the tree your source rather than an instrument, when those apples are eaten up you have nothing left. If you pay attention only to gathering the apples you'll be in bad shape. If you don't take care of the tree it will wither and die. It is the tree that produces the apples. The apples do not produce the tree. The apples come from the tree. In the same way, if you have a right relationship with God, and you make Him your Source, He will supply your needs either one way or some other way. He will use many, many instruments but He's teaching you to keep your mind upon Him. He's the Source.

Well, how can God make the fish jump into the net? I don't know how, but He can. It takes an act of faith. How can God give you a job when there are no jobs? I don't know how. He just can. How can God solve your marriage problems when you can't solve them and nobody else can solve them? I don't know but God *can* solve your marriage problems. God can give you a miracle if you'll give Him something to work with and then believe Him. God will not only give you what you need, He'll give it to you running over.

Now you watch this: Jesus says, "You launch out into the deep and let down your net for a catch." *There was a depth out there, a certain depth.*

THERE'S A DEPTH FOR YOUR GIVING

When I begin a project or I face a problem in my life, most of the time I try to solve it first by planting seed. It isn't always easy. Sometimes I forget. Sometimes the problem gets on top of me and all I can see is the problem and I don't put in the seed. But let me tell you, when I really get down serious with God, I start with a seed. I may start with something that I do.

Recently I had a problem and I did something for somebody. There's no way in the world I can ever get it back from them. They are the kind of people who always want something from you, but if you go back to them with a need they are going to tell you no. They are not going to do anything for you. But I was reminded when I had finished that they are not my Source. I am to do my giving without expecting anything back from the people I try to help. I am to expect something back from my Source. I am not to look to people anyway.

When I really get down to business with my problems and needs I try to remember my Source is God. Then I try to put a seed in. Even though it's tiny and small I try to do it. It does something for me.

Now I have a *depth*. The depth may be money I give or some of my time or some of my talent or some of my concern. That seed becomes my depth and I direct it toward my need. I don't know how God is going to meet the need, but when I put the seed in that's when I start knowing something *good* is going to happen to me. Some kind of a miracle or another of the *works* of God is going to happen in my life or through my life.

Well, the fishermen get a way out into the sea of Galilee at the proper depth and Jesus says, "Now, throw your nets over." And they threw them over. The God of the universe who scooped out the bed for the ocean and flung the stars from His fingertips, who created every living thing, spoke to His creatures—the fish of the sea—and said, "Strike that net; hit that net; fill that net." The fish heard the voice of their Creator and they hit the net. They filled it and began to slide over the top. The disciples got excited and began to pull the net in and it was so worn it began to break. Finally the boat was filled. It was so full it began to sink. They got . . .

A NET-BREAKING, BOAT-SINKING LOAD!

They had to call their partners over and they filled their boat. It was a miracle. It was another of the *works of God*.

Simon Peter saw the multiplication of the seed they had planted and he fell on his knees and said, "Lord, leave me. Leave me. I'm a sinful man. Lord, my ways have not been Your ways." (That's who a sinner is, one whose ways are not God's ways.)

And Jesus said, "No, I'm not going to leave you. You follow Me and I'll make you a fisher of men." He said, "Peter, leave off your old ways and take My ways. Become My disciple by following Me and then you'll be a fisher of men. You will have a concern for men. You will become a follower of Mine. You will be giving and the love of God will be flowing out of you."

Here is our Lord starting with a secular need and ending with a spiritual need and both of them are met. A man becomes a whole man. A man and his friends discover who their Source is—Christ. These men give their boat. They give out of their need and they see Christ take that seed and multiply it. These men are now in the presence of a miracle, a great work of God, that represents money for their families. It represents further employment and it represents more. This miracle says Jesus Christ is more reliable than any instrument, that He has more power over the sea of Galilee than the fishermen have over it.

THE SOURCE OF THE SEA OF GALILEE

By the way, I have visited the sea of Galilee many times. On one trip I went to a little place called Dan, which is so named in the Bible. There on the borders of Lebanon, I visited the spot where the Jordan River starts. It comes from a little spring out of the earth. It is a tiny little stream and it gets bigger and wider and deeper as it moves along. I followed the Jordan River as it started from its source until it became the sea of Galilee. Now the sea of Galilee empties out on the other side. It opens up on its other side and lets the river through. I drove around and saw it coming through and now it takes off again 60 or 80 miles, more or less, south, and it fills up another sea. But that sea has no outlet. It's called the Dead Sea. It doesn't give anything. The sea of Galilee just happily gives and receives, gives and receives. Its waters are fresh and full of fish, as indicated here by our Lord. I even ate fish caught from it while I was there. Then I went down to the Dead Sea and it is dead. Nothing can live in it because it has no outlet. It receives but doesn't give. The whole thing is a reminder of Seed-Faith.

Our Lord said, "Give, and it shall be given unto you." You may start small. I would say to anyone who would like to see if Seed-Faith works—start small. Take something out of your need. These men had an empty boat and it ended up full of fish. Maybe what you give won't even be the same thing you get back. You may receive back the same thing you give but I'll guarantee you one thing, there will be a lot more of it and it will be exactly what you need. It will have a tremendous spiritual effect upon you.

Peter now is amazed because the Source of his supply becomes the Lord of his life.

THE TROUBLE THAT WE HAVE WITH SEED-FAITH IS THAT WE WANT TO MAKE IT A GIM-MICK, WHEREAS OUR LORD WANTS IT TO BE-COME A WAY OF LIFE.

Seed-Faith is the opening up of oneself to God and to one's fellowman, and staying open with the love flowing out and God mutiplying it back in the form of our need. Your miracle begins in what you give, not in what you receive. What you give becomes something for God to work with and He does marvelous things with it. Giving becomes a way of life. You may start off small but you get deeper and wider and stronger in your heart. Your faith gets stronger and your needs are met more readily and you really become a Christian—a disciple or follower of Jesus Christ.

SUMMARY

THE MEANING OF THE MIRACLE CATCH OF FISH TO YOU IN THE NOW IS:

1. **Jesus Christ wants to redirect your thoughts from the past of futility and failure to the present of deliverance and success.** God wants you to be successful. God wants something good to happen to you (3 John 2).

2. **God has his own way of doing things . . .** He can make a way where there is no way . . . a job where there is no job . . . a supply where there is none.

3. **Seed-Faith is opening yourself up to God and to your fellowman.** It is giving of yourself—your love, time, concern, money, whatever you have—and letting God's love flow out of you to others in need. Seed-Faith is God multiplying your giving back to you in the form of your need.

4. **Seed-Faith begins with the need you have and brings you into a deeper involvement and participation with Christ until you truly become His Disciple.**

5

HOW YOU ARE
A PERSON TO CHRIST
AND THE MIRACLE HE OFFERS
FOR THE WHOLE MAN

And again he entered into Capernaum after some days; and it was noised that he was in the house. And straightway many were gathered together, insomuch that there was no room to receive them, no, not so much as about the door: and he preached the word unto them. And they came unto him, bringing one sick of the palsy, which was borne of four. And when they could not come nigh unto him for the press, they uncovered the roof where he was: and when they had broken it up, they let down the bed wherein the sick of the palsy lay. When Jesus saw their faith, he said unto the sick of the palsy, Son, thy sins be forgiven thee. But there were certain of the scribes sitting there, and reasoning in their hearts, Why doth this man thus speak blasphemies? Who can forgive sins but God only? And immediately when Jesus perceived in his spirit that they so reasoned within themselves, he said unto them, Why reason ye these things in your hearts? Whether is it easier to say to the sick of the palsy, Thy sins be forgiven thee; or to say, Arise, and take up thy bed, and walk? But that ye may know that the Son of man hath power on earth to forgive sins, (he saith to the sick of the palsy,) I say unto thee, Arise, and take up thy bed, and go thy way into thine house. And immediately he arose, took up the bed, and went forth before them all; insomuch that they were all amazed, and glorified God, saying, We never saw it on this fashion (Mark 2:1-12).

THIS MIRACLE is the story about a man who was paralyzed . . . a man who was brought to Jesus by four of his friends. But it is really much more than that. It is the story of Jesus Christ the Miracle-worker himself. This miracle shows us what the Father sent His Son to be:

GOD MADE HIS SON TO BE A PREACHER

We notice in Mark 12 that Jesus preached the Word unto them. And in Luke 4:18 Jesus himself said:

> *The Spirit of the Lord is upon me, because he hath anointed me to preach the gospel to the poor* (to those with needs) . . .

In the tenth chapter of Romans, verses 14 and 15, the Apostle Paul was saying, "How can they hear except they have a preacher? And how can he preach except he be sent of God?" In the same chapter Paul says:

> *Faith cometh by hearing, and hearing by the word of God* (Romans 10:17).

THE PREACHING OF THE WORD OF GOD HAS A VITALIZING EFFECT UPON A HUMAN BEING. FIRST, IT OPENS HIM UP TO THE POSSIBILITY OF GOD'S EXISTENCE. SECOND, IT CAUSES FAITH TO COME OUT OF HIM.

I grew up in Pontotoc County, Oklahoma, among the oilfields. When they first struck in our part of the state they would drill down into the earth. When they drilled down deep enough, the oil came forth. When I think about this statement, "Faith cometh by hearing, and hearing by the Word," I think of the oil coming up out of the ground. The oil had been there for centuries, lying undetected, undiscovered, and unused. In the same way, faith is in your heart. That faith may never have been tapped. You may have never even known it was there. Yet that faith is so powerful that if it were once released you would be truly a different human being. You would be vibrant, alive, effective, and come into the fullness of the career God has planned for you. This kind of faith *cometh*—it comes out of you as you hear the Word of God preached.

HOW IMPORTANT IS PREACHING?

It is important as life itself. How important is it to a preacher to preach? It is his life to preach. What must he preach? The same thing Christ preached: THE WORD. Not little pet theories or theological views, but the WORD. Jesus preached the Word unto them.

It's a very interesting fact that medical science is now taking into account the effect of the preaching of the gospel which inevitably produces a change of direction in a person's life. Recently I read a book by Dr. Karl Menninger, the famous psychiatrist from Topeka, Kansas. This book deals with the sense of sin. Dr. Menninger says that we Americans have lost our sense of sin. He says even we Christians have lost the sense of sin. He says preachers, as a general rule, are no longer preaching the gospel to the extent that people discover they have a sense of sin. He says without this sense of sin there can be no full healing of the human personality because when a person is engaged in wrong, such as being filled with bitterness toward others, having hate in his heart, of having something against another human being and hurting that person, or such as striking at God, and he feels that he isn't wrong—that it's OK to be like this, it's OK to commit sin—when he has no acute awareness that he is doing wrong, it is a deadly deterrent to health. He says we must recapture the sense of sin. We must repent.

Here is a doctor who is preaching repentance as much or more than most preachers do. Here is a man who is a medical doctor dealing primarily with the mind of a mortal and yet seeing that one's mind can be retarded spiritually, retarded by his own sinfulness for which he feels no awareness. Dr. Menninger says sin is a barrier. Finally he says:

> SIN IS A DEATH-DEALING DOSE OF POISON
> TO A PERSON'S INTELLECT . . .
> TO HIS BRAIN FUNCTIONING PROPERLY . . .
> TO HIS MENTAL HEALTH . . .

We usually think of health in terms of our bodies but we must learn to think of health in terms of our total self—mental health, physical health, spiritual health—health for the whole man. I have a surgeon friend and we talk about matters like this. In a recent conversation I talked to him about how he liked his patients to approach surgery. I asked him if there was a difference in the way people approach surgery. I asked if it made any difference to him.

He said, "It makes all the difference in the world. When I have a patient who has any degree of love for other people . . . when he is open to people . . . I can feel it. When he seems to be more loving, when he has confidence, it's really a pleasure to do surgery. I have a feeling myself that I'm going to be successful with him."

I said, "What do you do when you get a patient who thinks in the opposite way?"

"You mean a person full of bitterness?" he replied.

I said, "Yes."

He said, "I get lots of people like this who come for surgery. They are full of bitterness because they are ill. They are bitter because they haven't been able to get well. They are bitter at God. They are bitter at themselves. They are bitter at us physicians. They are bitter at—well, just about everything. They are just bitter. They don't come with a sense of faith that they can be cured. They just lie there like an inert mass. They are expecting miracles from the wrong source. I always have a sense of dread when I approach surgery with a person like this. While I'm not a preacher, I try to drop a subtle hint to that person that if he really wants the surgery to be successful . . . if he really wants to get well . . . he will have to *help* me to make him well."

FIRST, THE PREACHING OF THE WORD CAUSES A PERSON TO HAVE A SENSE OF SIN.

It makes us aware we are sinners. The Apostle Paul said, "I am a sinner saved by grace." He was so aware of having been a sinner that he still had the sense of being a sinner, although the grace of God had changed his life.

SECOND, THE PREACHING OF THE WORD CAUSES FAITH TO COME OUT OF OUR HEARTS.

I want you to think of your faith as being oil that must be drilled for and brought forth out of the ground. I want you to realize what the preaching of the gospel can do to you— it can reach down inside you and pull up that faith and cause it to come out of you.

I WANTED TO SOW MY "WILD OATS"...
I HAD NO SENSE OF SIN

At 17 years of age, lying dreadfully ill with tuberculosis, I was preached to by my own father who was a preacher. The truth is, I had been taken to church all my life and I had been preached to by scores of preachers.

There came a time that I wanted to get away from this. I wanted to sow my "wild oats." I felt I would change my life later on. But the facts of life are pretty cruel sometimes. Sickness slipped up on me and I was stricken. I learned I wasn't going to live much longer. For the first time my parents had a captive audience in me. I was lying there on the bed and couldn't get up. I lay there for five months. I really heard some preaching. I resented it at first but after a while I began to have a sense of sin in my life that I had done wrong.

Do you realize it never occurred to me before that I had done wrong, that the sins I'd committed were really *sins?* As a matter of fact, I never even thought about it. It was not a fact to me because I gave no credence to the fact that I had sinned. But as my parents read the Bible to me and shared with me, I couldn't go anywhere. I couldn't keep my ears shut up all the time. And this sense of sin came over me. Something else happened too. Faith began to come up out of me—faith that I *could* be saved from the sin in my life.

I'm absolutely confident that the preaching of the Word of God will give you a sense of sin. Secondly, it will bring the faith that's in you out of you. It doesn't need to be *in* you. It needs to be *out* of you. Someone says, "I have all the faith in the world." That's your trouble—you still have it! FOR FAITH TO BE EFFECTIVE, YOU HAVE TO RELEASE IT!

GOD MADE HIS SON A HEALER OF PERSONS...
JESUS PREACHED TO HEAL AND HE
HEALED TO PREACH

I tell you, I'm excited about this: **Jesus preached to heal and He healed to preach.** Someone said to me, "Don't you think it's nice for us preachers sometimes to preach just for ourselves, just to hear ourselves preaching?"

My reply is, "Just ask your church members about that."

"Well, why should we preach? To entertain ourselves? To entertain an audience?"

Well, our Lord Jesus Christ preached to *heal* and He healed to *preach* and here it is. What did God make His Son to be? First, God made Him a preacher but second, He made Him a healer of persons.

In this miracle we find Jesus preaching to a crowd that has filled the entire house, even the doorways. Suddenly the tiling on the roof—the ceiling—is being torn open. As Jesus looks up He sees some men peering down. He sees their faces. He sees a man on a little bed, a man who is paralyzed whom they have brought to be healed.

JESUS LOOKED UP AND SAW THEIR FAITH

He saw the faith of these four men, these four friends who were sowing seeds of faith. You never know when you sow a seed of faith how powerful it is. You never know when you give something just how great it will turn out to be. You never know how powerfully God will multiply it back!

YOUR SEED OF FAITH INDIVIDUALIZES YOU TO GOD

When you plant a seed of faith, when you go out of your way to help a human being or to contribute to a good cause—whatever it may be—that individualizes your faith to God. Christ *saw* THEIR faith.

As Jesus looked up, these men were looking down and they carefully let their friend down into the midst because they could not get him in through the doors. Now the man is lying there on the floor on his little bed. The crowd is watching every move and Jesus shows what He is. Remember, I said that Jesus preached to heal and He healed to preach. Looking at this man lying on the bed, He said, "Son, thy sins be forgiven thee . . . Arise, and take up thy bed, and go thy way into thine house."

You see, Jesus preached in order to heal a person but also He healed in order to preach. That is to say, the effect of His preaching was to bring a miraculous power upon a human life to change the entire person. The effect of His preaching was to change the entire person and the changing of that entire person became a sermon. It became the preaching of our Lord.

PREACHING HEALS AND HEALING
PREACHES . . .
HEALING DEMONSTRATES ALL OF GOD.

Why do so many people think Christianity is impotent, weak, and powerless—that it doesn't count in our society?

Because in so many places it has become empty words from our pulpits. It has become empty phrases from the people in the pews. It has become a charade, an outward form among us who claim to be Christians. So many of us are not involved with persons. Oh, we are involved with what our church teaches about its particular denominational emphasis. We are involved about being exclusive. We are Baptists. We are Methodists. We are Catholics. We are Pentecostals. We are Nazarenes. We are Lutherans, etc. But what about our being involved in the hurts and ills of human beings? How about our witness becoming healing and our healing becoming our witness? How about our Christianity becoming acts that touch human lives at the core—at their need—and the touching of those needs becoming our witness?

When my mother and father were telling me about having a sense of sin, that I should repent and ask God to forgive me of my sins, do you know what I was thinking? I was saying to myself, "Look, it's my lungs that hurt. My lungs need to be healed." Thank God, a little later they included the hurting of my lungs. They assured me that God was concerned about forgiving my sins *and* the healing of my bleeding lungs. How grateful I am for my parents—who are now with the Lord—who preached healing in the way that healing became their preaching.

I appreciate the renewal of the Holy Spirit that's beginning to come into the church. I am in the church and I'm not interested in leaving the church. I believe a much greater and far more widespread renewing is coming to the church. I believe we see signs of it on every side. Now is the time for people to see their mistakes and start correcting them. Now is the time not to blame one another but to help one another sow seeds of faith and to think about the healing of persons. You can preach the most beautiful sermon or give the most beautiful witness with your words that you have ever given, but unless it touches a life—unless a person is helped or healed or changed—just how valuable are your words?

You see, Jesus did not divide the spirit from the body. Jesus Christ looked upon the body as united with the soul. Jesus Christ looked at a human being as a person with a soul and a body. He didn't come to the person merely about his soul or merely about his body. I fear any kind of religion that dissects or divides a human being. I believe in the kind that makes the human being a whole person. Jesus said,

"Your *sins* are forgiven you . . . now take up your bed and walk." Here we see Christ getting the man into Seed-Faith.

Jesus is now directing the man's attention to the Source of his new life—God. (**Key #1: God is the Source of your total supply.**) The paralyzed man must find a Source for his life. The source he had in the past didn't work. He must find God. And he's finding Him. He's so thrilled that his friends are willing to bring him to Christ.

Now Jesus is dealing with the man's sins, with turning *his* life around. It is evident that the man was conscious of his sins or Jesus would not have touched him at that point. Jesus touched him at the very point where his thoughts were. He always does. Here He's dealing with a man who is conscious of his sins. Also, Jesus realizes that those sins are a hindrance. Evidently, the man, in making the trip to get there, is having a change of mind about his former way of life. He's ready to repent, which means to change one's mind. Jesus picked this up. Jesus is saying to him, "Those things you are doing wrong are hurting people. Now I want you to start giving. Start loving. Start caring and being concerned. Even though you are ill, you be concerned for some other ill person." (**Key #2: Seeding for your miracle: Put a seed of faith in FIRST.**)

James 5:16 says:

Pray one for another, that ye may be healed.

Then Jesus got him into expecting a miracle. (**Key #3: Expect a miracle.**) Jesus said, *"Take up thy bed . . .* take it up! Take that first step! Take that first step!!"

Do you know Jesus told him to take up his bed before the man was even healed? Jesus was drawing the faith out of him. He was causing his faith to come forth like oil comes out of the ground. He was telling him to take the first step. "TAKE THIS STEP. TAKE UP YOUR BED."

I can hear the man saying, "Look, I'm paralyzed. I can't move. I can't lift myself up." And Jesus saying back to him, "Well, if you can just wiggle one little finger, wiggle it. Move. Do something. Take the first step."

Someone said to me, "When God is ready to heal me, I'm ready."

I said, "You're two thousand years late! God's been ready all this time. God's been ready to heal your marriage, to heal your soul, to heal your mind, to heal your body, to heal your finances, to heal your problems all the time. He's waiting for you to take a step of faith, to move into Seed-Faith, to *act*."

God made His Son a preacher, a healer of persons and . . .

GOD MADE HIS SON A RESTORER OF FAMILIES

Jesus said, "Take up thy bed and go into *thine house*." Jesus Christ is concerned about your home—about father and mother and husband and wife and sons and daughters and children becoming united. Sickness cuts us down. Here in this story is a family whose breadwinner is paralyzed. Here is a family where the bills are piling up. Here is a family who today would have been forced to have been on welfare. Here is a father who is in a condition that he can't help. And Jesus healed him and sent him home to his family.

Jesus sent the paralyzed man home—a whole man—able now to care for his family, to be the father God intended him to be. No longer did the family have to fear being torn apart because of the lack of finances, or to be on welfare. Now they had a father who was well, a father who could once again care for them.

SUMMARY

THE MEANING OF THE HEALING OF THE PARA-
LYZED MAN TO YOU IN THE NOW IS:

1. The preaching of the Word of God opens you up to
    the possibility of God's existence.
         It causes faith to come out of you.
         It causes you to have a sense of sin.

2. Jesus is concerned about your whole life.
         He wants to forgive your sins, to turn your life
         around.
             He wants to do a work of God in your life—
             to give you the miracle you need.

3. Jesus is concerned about your family.
         He wants to restore that which is broken—to mend
         broken relationships—to renew the love that has
         seemingly died—to replenish you financially.

6

HOW THROUGH CHRIST'S MIRACLES—WHEN YOU ARE FEELING THE WORST OF THE WORST—ALL IS NOT LOST

And as he entered into a certain village, there met him ten men that were lepers, which stood afar off: And they lifted up their voices, and said, Jesus, Master, have mercy on us. And when he saw them, he said unto them, Go shew yourselves unto the priests. And it came to pass, that, as they went, they were cleansed. And one of them, when he saw that he was healed, turned back, and with a loud voice glorified God, And fell down on his face at his feet, giving him thanks: and he was a Samaritan. And Jesus answering said, Were there not ten cleansed? but where are the nine? There are not found that returned to give glory to God, save this stranger. And he said unto him, Arise, go thy way: thy faith hath made thee whole (Luke 17:12-19).

ALL OF US FEEL PAIN . . . we experience isolation . . . loneliness. We feel cut off and burdened down. We face problems that are overwhelming. Sometimes we feel like we are not going to make it. We may even feel our situation is worse than what anyone else has ever faced. We are individuals and each of us is unique in our personality and irreplaceable in our person.

Some of us have a higher pain threshold than others. Some are inclined toward depression. Others seem to be born in the sunshine. They are cheery all their lives without apparently even trying. As individuals, we have to face the things we encounter in life in our own individual ways. The message of this miracle is that Christ comes to each individual . . . and He comes to do a WORK OF GOD in even the worst possible situations. The miracle of the cleansing of the ten lepers says to you:

1. ALTHOUGH THE WORST OF THE WORST IS HAPPENING TO YOU—ALL IS NOT LOST!

At the time this miracle occurred, leprosy was considered the worst of the worst. These men had been expelled from their communities because leprosy was considered very contagious. It was a horrible disease and there was no cure . . . no medicine such as we have today. A leper was required by law to cry out, "Unclean, unclean" if someone approached him who was unaware of his disease.

Lepers suffered the loss of all family ties. They suffered terrible isolation from other human beings. Sometimes they lived in groups outside the city. They made their homes wherever they could, sometimes in a cave. They were literally outcasts.

CHRIST WAS APPROACHABLE BY THE WORST OF THE WORST

When they called out to him in their hideous forms He listened, He heard, and He stopped for their approach. Probably there's nothing comparable today in the way this disease works upon the body unless it would be cancer, as the worst of the worst, particularly certain forms of it we face today.

I especially remember praying for a certain terminally ill man in one of our crusades. When I reached him there was an odor that I had never experienced before and involuntarily I drew back and began throwing up. Before I even knew what I was doing I was saying to myself, "No, no, no, no, no!" And inside I felt God rebuking me. He was saying to me, "If you are not willing to pray for this man, you are not worthy to be a Christian."

It upset me and frightened me so much until I went right back to that man. I remember then that the odor no longer bothered me. When I had made up my mind that I, a Christian, was going to do what Christ had called me to do, then I was able to minister to him. After I'd prayed for him he put his arms around me and tears rolled down his cheeks. He wanted not only to be healed . . . he wanted to feel the touch of a loving hand. He wanted another human being to be near him, somebody who would pray. I don't know how much help he received (we had no further contact with him) but I know I received a lot from the experience.

Now what do you do with the worst of the worst? What do you do when you are experiencing something in your life or the life of a loved one, say a member of the family or someone extremely dear to you, that is absolutely beyond your control—beyond the pale of human power? What do you do when your need can't be touched by medicine or anything else you know about?

Strangely enough, the problem may be a marital problem. It may be a husband and wife who are growing apart and the break seems so big until it is the worst of the worst. It may be a runaway child, an uncurable illness or financial hardship. It's strange how life's overwhelming experiences can make you feel it is the worst of the worst.

I'd like to ask you a personal question: What are you personally enduring right now? And *enduring* is the word. I know that whatever it is, it is a terrifying experience and yet I tell you, all is not lost!

When these men who had the worst of the worst diseases—leprosy—saw Christ, they cried out to Him and said, "Jesus (or Master), have mercy on us." They *asked*. They *called* upon Jesus.

They went from the raw edge to the center.

> They went from the perimeter to the very heart of
> the possibility of a cure.
> They asked for mercy.

They did not ask for justice. They asked for mercy. The way they asked was a confession itself. It was a confession that they had gone beyond their own strength. It was a confession to the way of life they had lived prior to their illness which required an act of mercy for their souls to be cleansed as well as their bodies. They said, "Have mercy on *us*."

HOW DO YOU APPROACH GOD?

Many people have said to me that they don't know how to talk to God. One man even said, "Mr. Roberts, I've never asked God for anything." He told me how old he was and said that not once in his life had he ever asked God to do anything for him. Apparently he felt like a tiny speck in this universe and that God was millions of miles removed, completely aloof from his existence. This man had never met God.

Do you feel a reluctance in talking to God? Is there a certain awesomeness about God that has a more or less terrifying effect on you and causes you to withdraw within yourself? Well, that's not unusual. Many people feel this way. I've felt it too to some extent. Even now there are times that I have a rather awesome feeling when I think about God. But this is the great reason why Jesus came.

JESUS CAME TO PERSONALIZE AND INDIVIDUALIZE GOD . . .

HE CAME TO SHOW US WHAT GOD IS LIKE.

One of the greatest statements our Lord ever made that means the most to you and to me right now is this:

The Son can do nothing of himself, but what he seeth the Father do (John 5:19).

When you think of the life of Christ, His life of healing and salvation, of His extension of mercy toward human beings, you can see that this is Jesus saying, "That's what I saw My Father do." Through the centuries His Father was extending himself to humanity if they would only receive it and there emerged great miracles of compassion toward people. When you read the Old Testament you see remarkable instances of God intervening in time and space and touching a human being—sparing a life or performing some outstanding miracle that benefited a person, or a family, or a group of people, or the entire human race. And Jesus said, "I do only what I see my Father do." So when we think of Jesus we are to think of God himself, because Jesus is the real true manifestation of God.

JESUS IS GOD WALKING AMONG US—
HE IS GOD SITTING WHERE WE SIT . . .
FEELING WHAT WE FEEL . . . AND
EXPERIENCING WHAT WE EXPERIENCE

I know it is not easy to grasp that Jesus sits where you sit . . . He feels what you feel . . . He experiences what you experience . . . and He was tempted in all points like you are. No, it isn't always easy.

Some time ago I said on my television program: "Have you ever felt lust? Well, Jesus felt it too." Then I asked several other questions and said, "Jesus felt that." Later I received a letter from a person who said, "Do you actually mean that Jesus Christ our Savior felt lust? How can that be?"

I wrote back that had Jesus not felt everything we feel, He could not have known what we go through. That doesn't mean that he yielded to lust. He did *not,* but He felt it just like anybody else feels lust. The difference is He overcame it. Jesus moved among people and as He did He experienced temptations. There isn't a temptation you have that Jesus did not have. He was "tempted like as we are, yet without sin" (Hebrews 4:15). The devil threw it at Him just like he throws it at you. That's the remarkable thing about God sending His Son in the flesh. Jesus Christ, your Savior, experienced what you experience. He knows what you are going through. He *understands* and He *loves* you. **Jesus loves you!**

GOD LOVES YOU!!

The one thing the typical human being does not realize is, *"God loves me."* Maybe you think He loves someone else . . . but you?? I admit that when you are going through a terrible experience it's hard to think that *anybody* loves you. But somehow God wants to break through to you—to let you know He loves you.

Some time ago at the conclusion of a chapel service at Oral Roberts University, a young girl came up to me. She took my hand and said, "Today is the first day I ever knew God loves me. Something in this chapel service reached out to me and all of a sudden I just *knew* God loved ME."

All is not lost. You may think, "Well, it's over. I've had it. Nothing can be done now." That's the way we talk. And these lepers certainly knew this kind of language. They not only talked it, they also experienced it. But when they saw the Lord Jesus Christ they realized all was not lost.

Can you realize the existence of Jesus Christ, that He really exists, that He's concerned about you? Do you realize you can call upon Him—you can *ask?* In fact, you *should* ask! The Bible says:

> *Ask, and it shall be given you; seek, and ye shall find; knock, and it shall be opened unto you* (Matthew 7:7).

> *Ye have not, because ye ask not* (James 4:2).

Don't be backward in asking largely of God. Here are these men who saw Christ, and even though they were quite a distance from Him they lifted up their voices and cried, "Master, have mercy on us." I've often said, "As long as there's one breath in your body you still have hope," because God is always at the point of your need. These lepers were standing afar off from Jesus with their need of healing and cleansing from leprosy, yet when they called, "Master, have mercy upon us," He was there. There He was! And whatever your need is right now—in the NOW—He is there. He is there. Christ is there at the point of your need.

The second thing this miracle says to you is:

2. YOUR FAITH IS IN YOUR OBEDIENCE

Faith is in obedience. Jesus said, *"Go show yourselves* to the priests." Now that was not a brush-off, even though it might have appeared to be. This was part of the healing process under the Law of Moses. When a person recovered from something like leprosy he had to return to the priest. The priest would examine him, looking for blemishes, and when he found nothing wrong he would pronounce the person *clean.* It was a form of medicine as we would term medicine today. It was a secular thing within a spiritual setting. It was something that was a part of the Law of Moses which was not necessarily spiritual in its content, but had spiritual overtones.

It reminds us . . .

JESUS JOINED THE SECULAR AND THE SPIRITUAL.

I've said that countless times in my ministry to thousands and millions of people. I think it's important for us not to separate the secular from the spiritual. It is important to realize that whatever is of a helpful nature is ordained of God, whether it is a gift of medical science or a gift of healing through prayer. These things are not to be separated—they are to be joined together. Jesus indicates at least part of this by saying, "Go show yourselves to the priests." There was something He wanted them to *do*.

As they went, they were cleansed. The process of cleansing began to happen as they *went* . . . step by step . . . to the priest to whom Jesus sent them to be examined and pronounced clean. As they made that journey, a cleansing of the leprosy began in them.

HEALING IS A PROCESS

A miracle may seem to take only a moment but usually it has been in the process for days or weeks or even months. I used to think that when I prayed for someone and the healing didn't happen immediately that my prayers had failed, or something was wrong. But often I would hear from that person later that something had happened, but it had not necessarily been completed in that moment. God's time is not always our time . . . but His time is always the best time. I personally believe a gradual healing is better than an instant one because you prepare yourself mentally and spiritually both to receive it AND to keep it. GOD IS NEVER TOO EARLY AND GOD IS NEVER TOO LATE.

Obedience is in our faith and our faith is in our obedience. That is, you have to have an obedient spirit. This is part of faith itself. Your faith has to take action. You have to get with it. You have to focus yourself upon God and determine in your heart to do His will. These men had to turn right around and go to the priest which they were not accustomed to doing. These men had been expelled by society. Now this Stranger is saying, "Go back into society . . . go back into the church . . . go back to the leaders of the church and shew yourself."

And they obeyed. What if they had not obeyed? Remember, Jesus didn't say, "I'm going to heal you." He only said, "Go . . ." I think it took a lot of faith for these men to obey and to make that trip. But faith is in obedience. You can't have faith without obedience. As they obeyed . . . as they WENT . . . they were healed.

WE MUST ALL LEARN OBEDIENCE . . .
ONE WAY OR ANOTHER

Reverend Tommy Tyson, our first chaplain at Oral Roberts University, tells the story of the remarkable training process of the Arabian horse in the Middle East. As you know, only recently has a mechanized form of travel been available in the Middle East, in the Arabian deserts. There are hundreds of miles of trackless deserts in those countries and in the past the Arabian horse was the way many people traveled. In many instances, they still travel that way today.

Tommy said in order for the Arabian horse to become a highly regarded horse, a horse of great quality and of great price, it had to go through a very special schooling. He said the trainer would put the horse through all types of tests, but there was one test that was the most severe. As it came near the time for the graduation of the horse, the trainer would withhold water from it. He would have the horses do without water as long as they could without dying of thirst. You can imagine what those horses were enduring in the 130-degree heat of those deserts, going for days without a drink of water. All the while, the trainer is leading these horses to water. Of course, as they draw near the water they can smell it. As they draw near they break loose, and with the last strength they have they run to the water to plunge in. Just as they get there, the trainer blows his whistle. The horses that stop without drinking, turn around and trot back to the trainer, graduate. They are perfectly obedient horses.

Now why is such a test . . . such an obedience . . . necessary? Because the life of the man on that horse is entrusted to the horse. Imagine yourself out on the trackless desert on the back of a disobedient horse, a horse who will not obey the signals you give him. You could both die.

Tommy Tyson, in telling that story, said that Christianity is tough. It's not easy. It was not intended to be easy, because man has to learn obedience. If he does not learn to obey God, he will obey man or he will obey the devil. He will learn some kind of discipline whether he wants to or not. He may have to learn it by the law and there are many men behind prison walls today who are being subjected to the learning of discipline. Whether they willingly obey or not, they obey. So each one of us has to learn for himself the meaning of Christ's word:

> *If any man will come after me* (be my disciple),
> *let him deny himself, and take up his cross daily,*
> *and follow me* (Luke 9:23).

FOLLOW ME. We must become sensitive to the promptings of the Holy Spirit, open-minded to whatever the Lord would have us do. Sometimes we are so dense. We don't seem to know God is speaking to us . . . that He is giving us a signal. We come right up to drinking the water, like the horse did, and hear the whistle blowing. This means that God would have us draw back and endure a little longer. He has a greater purpose. He's preparing us for something that's greater than we've ever conceived.

This is why so many people break down in the crisis. They cannot serve because they've not had the discipline. They cannot achieve their goals because they break down in the discipline. We see this in athletics all the time. We see it in college players who would go on to the pros. Some have built into themselves a discipline that they carry beyond the athletic floor. Those that don't, never make it or if they start they are cut from the squad.

The same is true in business. Anybody can start a business but not everybody can complete one.

The same is also true in marriage. Just about anyone can get a license . . . and get married, but the test is after the ceremony. It's whether discipline has been learned . . . whether we are sensitive and open to one another or not. I think one of the greatest lessons in this miracle of the healing of the ten lepers is that faith is in obedience.

My mother, who went to be with the Lord some months ago, gave me the greatest advice I ever had. She said, "Son, stay little in your own eyes." I'm sure she gave me that advice because she knew that would be a difficult assignment for me. She said, "Stay little in your own eyes and God will bless the world through you." And then she gave me a second piece of advice. She said, "Oral, always obey God." Now my mother didn't say that to me one or two or three times. She said that to me constantly over a great many years. And just a few hours before she slipped away, she said those same words to me again: "Son, stay little in your own eyes and obey God."

The third great meaning I see in this miracle for you is that you can have . . .

3. A COMPLETED MIRACLE

Jesus showed us what a completed miracle is. The ten lepers were cleansed *as they went.* One of them—when he saw he was healed—stopped, turned around, and came back to Jesus. He cried out with a loud voice, glorifying God. Then he fell upon his face before Jesus and worshiped Him.

A COMPLETED MIRACLE IS A PERSON WITH A THANKFUL HEART WHO KNOWS HE GOT MORE THAN HE DESERVED.

So many times we think we don't get what we deserve, that others are benefited more than we are. We wind up with an unthankful heart and often a bitter spirit. I've often said, "The worst thing that can ever happen to a human being is to develop a bad attitude." When this happens, nothing is right. The food isn't right. The marriage isn't right. The job isn't right. The lessons in class aren't right. The game isn't right. Nothing is right if one has a bad attitude. When this happens the only thing you can do is to submit your attitude to Christ. Admit it, confess it, and bring it to Christ. Say, "God, I have a bad attitude. I repent of it. God give me a good attitude. Give me Your Spirit."

Here is a man who had a thankful heart because he realized he got more than he deserved. This leper got *more* than the healing of his body. This is very important. He was healed of more than leprosy. Jesus said, "There were ten cleansed, where are the nine? There's only one who has come back and he's a stranger." Then He said to this man, "Go thy way, thy faith hath made thee whole." Now notice this, as the ten went they were cleansed of their leprosy. The leprosy left their bodies. But in this one man, not only did the leprosy leave his body but he himself also was made WHOLE by his faith. The whole man was touched by his obedience to Christ's healing command and he received a completed miracle.

When I was ill I not only had tuberculosis but also I was a stutterer. All the while my parents were trying to get me to be saved, to get my soul fixed up, I kept wanting my tongue healed from stuttering and my lungs healed from tuberculosis. I couldn't understand why they were concerned about my salvation when I was hurting and dying with tuberculosis. But they were wiser than I was. They knew I needed complete healing. They were desperate for me to be healed from tuberculosis. They were praying that I might get healed, but they knew the real answer would begin with my soul being made right with God. Then, hopefully, my body would be right and it would be healed. Thank God, I got both.

Oh, I still have a little stammering left. I stumble over some words once in a while. I remember once when I was addressing a group of university students at the College of the Pacific in Stockton, California. There were maybe a thousand students there and we were having a great time. All of a sudden I stuttered some and a student stood up and said, "Hey, Mister, you said you were healed of stuttering."

The only thing I could say was, "I guess God has left enough of it to remind me that without Him I can't talk at all."

There are many things about this miracle of our Lord healing the lepers that impress me but I think the greatest of all is . . .

ONE OF THE TEN FOUND CHRIST AS THE SOURCE FOR HIS LIFE.

The other nine got a physical healing. There's no doubt about it. Do you know in medical science there are medical miracles? I mean today there are such miracles in surgery and in medicine. People can and do recover from diseases. Years ago this was thought completely impossible in many such cases. Some of those people who recover never give God thanks. They never think of it as a spiritual thing that they received, that it's part of the gifts of God to them. It never humbles them. It never causes them to be closer to God. It doesn't even make them think of God.

Jesus was astonished and He said, "Were there not ten?"

"Yes, there were ten."

"Well, where are the nine? They received a healing but they have no Source for their life. Really, they don't know God and may never know God. Where are the nine?" Then He said to the one who returned to give thanks, "Thy faith hath made thee whole."

You see, this leper discovered a Source for his life. He had something that went beyond the recovery of his body. He now would have Someone with him always. He would have Someone to whom he could turn in the days ahead when something else got bad. He would have Someone to praise and to thank day by day. This man was no longer a leper—he was a whole man. And he had a Source for his life.

SUMMARY

WHATEVER YOUR SITUATION MAY BE TODAY, KNOW THIS:

1. **All is not lost!**

   Your problem may be too great for any human power to solve but it is not bigger than God. And God is there with you—at the point of your need—and He is saying, "I know how you feel and I am concerned. I LOVE YOU. And I can and will help you."

2. **Faith is in obedience.**

   Obedience is in our faith and our faith is in our obedience. You have to have an obedient spirit. Your faith has to take action. You have to focus upon God and determine in your heart to do His will. Whatever God says to you (whatever you feel He is saying to you deep in your heart), do it!

3. **You can have a completed miracle!**

   A completed miracle is a person with a thankful heart who knows he got more than he deserved. When your miracle comes—and it will—don't forget to thank God your Source for that miracle. You may find God through the need that you are facing right now. But when that need is met, don't stop there. Go on and make God the Source of your total life! Know that you now have Someone you can turn to at any time . . . anywhere. Cultivate a thankful heart.

7

THE REMARKABLE WAY
YOU AND CHRIST AND HIS MIRACLES
BELONG TOGETHER—ALWAYS

And when he had sent the multitudes away, he went up into a mountain apart to pray: and when the evening was come, he was there alone. But the ship was now in the midst of the sea, tossed with waves: for the wind was contrary. And in the fourth watch of the night Jesus went unto them, walking on the sea. And when the disciples saw him walking on the sea, they were troubled, saying, It is a spirit; and they cried out for fear. But straightway Jesus spake unto them, saying, Be of good cheer; it is I; be not afraid. And Peter answered him and said, Lord, if it be thou, bid me come unto thee on the water. And he said, Come. And when Peter was come down out of the ship, he walked on the water, to go to Jesus. But when he saw the wind boisterous, he was afraid; and beginning to sink, he cried, saying, Lord, save me. And immediately Jesus stretched forth his hand, and caught him, and said unto him, O thou of little faith, wherefore didst thou doubt? And when they were come into the ship, the wind ceased. Then they that were in the ship came and worshipped him, saying, Of a truth thou art the Son of God (Matthew 14:23-33).

(Mark 6:48-52 gives slightly more information concerning this miracle of Jesus:)

And he saw them toiling in rowing; for the wind was contrary unto them: and about the fourth watch of the night he cometh unto them, walking upon the sea, and would have passed by them. But when they saw him walking upon the sea, they supposed it had been a spirit, and cried out: For they all saw him, and were troubled. And immediately he talked with them, and saith unto them, Be of good cheer: it is I; be not afraid. And he went up unto them into the ship; and the wind ceased: and they were sore amazed in themselves beyond measure, and wondered. For they considered not the miracle of the loaves: for their heart was hardened.

WHAT IS THE MEANING to you of the miracle of Jesus walking on the water? What application can you make of it in your daily life? When you are facing some storm of your existence . . . when you are hemmed in within the circumference of your daily life . . . and you are not accustomed to God intervening in miraculous ways to help you come through that problem or need, just what do you do?

ARE YOU AWARE OF THE POSSIBILITY OF A MIRACLE?

Or have you separated Jesus from miracles? Is He the Christ, but separate and apart from the performance of miracles? Do you wonder if there are miracles at all? Or if there are miracles, do you feel they come from a source other than Jesus Christ? What is there in this story . . . this miracle . . . that exists for you in the now?

First of all, I think you should notice an extraordinary happening, and that is the hardening of the hearts of these disciples. These twelve men had followed Christ from the very beginning. Now Jesus tells them to get into a ship and go to the other side of the sea while He goes apart in the mountain to pray. Now while He is up there praying and they're rowing across the sea of Galilee a storm strikes of such magnitude that their lives are in danger.

In the fourth watch of the night—which was between three and six o'clock in the morning—Jesus Christ left His hillside of prayer. He came to the water's edge, and having no boat He simply stepped on the waters which became a liquid pavement beneath his feet and he began to walk. I mean it's the most astonishing thing that you could ever conceive of. Jesus simply was unstoppable. He *walked* on the water. The waves didn't stop Him. The winds that were blowing the ship apart couldn't touch Him. He was like the eye of the storm itself, a place of central calm. Edward Markham, the poet, said of the cyclone, "At the heart of the cyclone tearing the sky . . . is a place of central calm."

Here Jesus is perfectly balanced upon the waves—the winds and waters unable to touch Him. The law of gravity is unable to pull Him down. He is walking . . . and He walks *all* the way. Soon He gets near enough that they can see Him. He's like a silhouette there in the moonlight. Perhaps when the lightning strikes He's illumined and they see something which to them looks like an apparition. They cried, "It's a spirit! It's a ghost."

Across the waves came Jesus' clear compelling voice, "Be of good cheer. It is I. Be not afraid."

But they *were* afraid. Despite the fact that Jesus told who He was and for them not to be afraid, they *were*. One of them in the ship cried, "If you are the Christ, bid me come to you."

Christ said, "Come."

And this disciple, Peter, took some steps on the water. He actually walked a few steps on the water. Then he got his eyes off Jesus and, momentarily, on the storm itself. He began to sink and called for help. Christ stretched forth his hand, caught him, and together they walked to the ship. The wind ceased and it was as if there had been no storm at all.

Now, they're on the shore. The disciples are astonished. They look upon Christ in awe. They're thunderstruck. It's really unbelievable. Mark, in his Gospel, adds something like a postscript. He says, "For they considered not the miracle of the loaves: for their heart was hardened."

Now how in the world can you go through such an episode as this—actually seeing Christ subduing the billowing waves and making them a pavement beneath His feet, walking on the water and stilling the storm—without believing? He even enabled one of the disciples to walk on the water. It is a miracle of fantastic proportions. But their hearts are hardened. They could not put Christ and miracles together. And that's the first thought I want to share with you:

1. CHRIST AND MIRACLES AND YOU
BELONG TOGETHER

I feel this is the most difficult problem we have . . . the problem of believing that Christ and miracles and you belong together. Yes, it's true. The disciples were there at Jesus' first miracle at Cana of Galilee where He turned the water into wine. When they saw that great miracle they believed on the Lord. It was clearly described, "This beginning of miracles did Jesus." The beginning. As they followed along with Jesus from place to place they saw Him do more and more of the *works of the Father*—miracles. They saw Him take a little boy's lunch of a few loaves and fishes and multiply it to feed five thousand hungry men. They even took part in it. Yet, as Jesus continued doing the works of the Father, one after the other, they finally reached a place where their hearts were hardened. That is, they were no longer in a position to associate them with the lordship of Jesus Christ. There was a breakdown in their belief that Christ and miracles were of the same distinct power of God working among men.

When Christ turned the water into wine at Cana of Galilee, His first miracle, they believed on Him.

Now, when He walks on the water, they're frightened.

They can't even recognize Him as the same Christ. After the miracle has taken place and their lives are spared in a manner that's beyond comprehension, they're awestruck but their hearts are hardened. They are not able to accept it as an ongoing part of the Lord's work in their lives.

Now why?

I think it was because they didn't understand yet that Jesus Christ had come to do the works of His Father . . . that He came to do only what He had seen His Father do. Jesus said:

> *The Son can do nothing of himself, but what he seeth the Father do: for what things soever he doeth, these also doeth the Son likewise* (John 5:19).
>
> *I must work the works of him that sent me* (John 9:4).

Jesus called miracles *the works of the Father*. There are references in the Gospels to the fact that they were miracles, but when Jesus talked about them He talked about them primarily in terms of the works of God—the ordinary workings of God.

God doing His thing in life may be considered extraordinary by people—or a miracle—but it is ordinary to God. It is not something big God is doing—it is simply God being himself, extending and expressing His love and concern for human beings, coming to them at the point of their needs, coming to them where a miracle has to happen or they will be destroyed in some way.

I don't think enough people understand that today. Perhaps you don't understand that Christ and miracles and you belong together—ALWAYS. Just as the people in New Testament times were frightened by a miracle, you may be frightened. I've prayed for hundreds and even thousands of people who were literally shaking when prayer was offered for them.

Every Sunday morning there are pastors who stand in their pulpits and say, "So-and-so of our church are in the hospital; would you pray for their recovery?"

Is this a form that they are going through, or do they really believe that prayer can bring about recovery? Is the idea of a miracle simply a part of our formal religion, or is it an actual occurrence that we expect from God and believe for in the now of our needs and problems? If we can settle this one problem in the church, I believe the church would undergo an overnight change that would put it upon the cutting edge of human need immediately. Throughout this nation and the world there would be supernatural deliverances of human beings of such magnitude that the eyes of billions would be focused upon the Son of God, the King of kings and the Lord of lords.

I believe broken lives would be restored.

I believe blind eyes would be opened and deaf ears unstopped.

I believe cancers would fall out of people's bodies.

I believe marriages that have been falling apart would erupt in love. And the husband and wife would love each other like they never have before.

I believe that children would be reunited with their parents and the family would become a whole family.

I believe that we would do exploits in the name of Christ. We would start a career and nothing could stop us. We would start a business and it would prosper.

I believe that from one end of the land to the other there would be miracle after miracle and people would understand that God is in our midst.

If this happened, we would not go sit in our church pews on Sunday morning and listen to the choir and the preacher and then walk out as if nothing had happened. I mean, we would be excited!! We wouldn't be able to wait until the church doors opened. We would expect Jesus Christ to be there. And if Jesus Christ were there, He would be walking on the water to us in our storm which is engulfing us.

The second meaning of this miracle to you is that:

2. JESUS WANTED THE DISCIPLES TO UNITE THE SPIRITUAL AND THE SECULAR IN THEIR DAILY LIVES

The circumference of their daily existence was the sea of Galilee. A little place of water about six miles wide and

14 miles long dotted by little towns around it. Now that was the circumference of their existence; that was where they spent their daily lives.

Their working hours were spent at the edge of the water, or mostly on the water, because they were fishermen by trade. The sea of Galilee was something they had to contend with. Often its waters would roll over them in a storm. The wind would turn boisterous almost instantly. The sea of Galilee is situated 'below sea level and storms strike without warning. In ten mintues' time a storm of such power that could destroy the boats built at that time, could come up from seemingly nowhere.

Every time these fishermen went out on the sea of Galilee they were taking their lives into their hands. Their lives were spent there daily. On many occasions the sea would refuse to give up its resources—its fish—of which they made their living. In their daily existence they had a problem of relating the spiritual to the secular—of seeing God coming from His mountain of prayer down to the stormy waves where they were trying to make a living, or about to be destroyed by the elements.

One woman said, "The trouble with life is it's so daily." And it's true. These little daily things that we wrestle with can really crush us. I think we're sometimes more prepared to face a terrible event than we are the continuous little things that go bad day after day—the things that we face every morning. For instance, the mother in the home having to take care of the children every day and cook breakfast every morning and wash the dishes every day and clean the house every day.

In the same way, the husband has to go to work and do the same job. The student has to go to class every day. All of us have to do something every day and face the little petty annoyances until the circumference of our existence narrows. Within that little cell-like human existence the daily things of our lives hurt us, upset us, irritate us, and tear us apart. We forget God is concerned even with the daily things of our lives.

Sure, the disciples could understand that Christ wanted to go up into the mountain and spend the night in prayer. That was a *spiritual* communion. They could accept that. What they could not accept was that He was leaving that mountaintop to come down to them in this daily problem they were facing with the sea of Galilee.

The same is true of us today. Sure, we can think of Jesus off somewhere. Various ones think of Him at the right hand of the Father or in Heaven.

Maybe they'll find Him in the Bible or they'll hear Him preached about in a sermon at church, or they'll read a good article, or they'll hear a song. People tend to think of Jesus in terms like these. And it's terribly hard to unite the secular with the spiritual—to understand that Jesus Christ invades the secular. But the secular is HIS.

JESUS UNITES THE SECULAR WITH THE SPIRITUAL. WHATEVER YOU FACE IN THE SECULAR IS AS DEAR TO HIM AS WHAT YOU FACE IN THE SPIRITUAL BECAUSE YOU ARE BOTH PHYSICAL AND SPIRITUAL AND ALL OF YOU IS HIS PROPERTY (1 Corinthians 6:19,20).

He made you the way you are. That is to say, God made you spiritual and physical.

My mother-in-law said that during a hard period of their lives when they were raising eight children, they would sometimes run out of groceries. They had a barrel where they kept their flour. She is a very dedicated Christian and she said it was difficult to look into that empty flour barrel and say, "Praise the Lord."

I think it is just as difficult today to reach into your pocket where there's no money and say, "Praise the Lord." Or to have a handful of bills that you can't pay and say, "Praise the Lord." Or to have something going wrong in the marriage and say, "Praise the Lord." I think it's difficult to bring Christ into the problems we face in our daily existence.

It certainly was for these disciples. Yet our Lord, in the fourth watch of the night—when the natural forces were at their lowest ebb, when they were at the greatest danger point—left the mountainside and came to them. I cannot say too much about that because I think it's so important to people today to understand that Jesus Christ *really* sits where you sit . . . feels what you feel . . . and experiences what you do.

Several of my friends have said to me, "Why do you keep saying that Jesus Christ feels what you feel, He sits where you sit, He experiences what you experience?"

First, I think I say it primarily for myself because it's hard for me to remember. Second, I say it because I think people need to hear it said. You need to hear it said. You need to remember it. Maybe you won't remember it today or tomorrow but perhaps the next day you will. Maybe in a moment when all seems lost, it will come back. Perhaps when you are hurting you will remember, "Jesus sat here. Jesus felt what I feel. Jesus experienced what I'm experiencing. He was tempted in every point like I am." Jesus was a man who came down to earth. He was God but He was also man.

Oooh . . . think of taking the secular, material, part of your life and uniting it with the spiritual!! Think of feeling the same openness to ask Christ to help you in both so that you don't separate the secular from the spiritual . . . so that you bring whatever is hurting you to God . . . so you are not reticent or reluctant about either one! Whether it is a spiritual problem or physical problem you know that Jesus Christ is concerned.

I think the third meaning of this miracle is:

3. JESUS ALWAYS COMES TO YOU AT THE POINT OF YOUR NEED

It's remarkable what Jesus did that night. He was on the mountain praying. He had just performed a tremendous miracle of turning a little boy's lunch into a huge amount of food to feed five thousand men. Now you would think He would have been so exalted and triumphant over that, He would have wanted to go somewhere and celebrate. But He went away to pray.

WHEN YOU HAVE A GREAT SUCCESS, THAT'S WHEN YOU NEED TO BE CAREFUL

Apparently when you have a great success, you're almost immediately struck by the devil. That's the time you need to be the most careful. You see, you are pretty careful when things are going bad. You're reaching out and hoping God will come. You usually get real serious. But when you have a great experience with God you tend to think you had so much to do with it that you get puffed up.

I think it's wonderful that Jesus, after this triumph, went apart into the mountain to pray.

The wife of one of the ORU coaches received the Holy Spirit recently. It was a remarkable experience of the Lord really working in her life but she was astonished to find how the devil immediately attacked her. It seemed like everything went wrong. She couldn't understand why everything didn't calm down and get real quiet after having received the Holy Spirit. She couldn't understand why everybody was not reacting kindly to her. She even found herself getting irritated with her loved ones. Then someone reminded her that when you receive something from God the devil *always* comes to attack you. And she began to realize what was happening and made a readjustment in her thinking that was very helpful to her—and to others.

I know I have to be careful along this line. For example, when I think I've taught or preached well, very few people seem to think I did. When I think I have not done well, then people usually come up and tell me how well I did. I think that is because God is trying to keep me where He wants me . . . as humble as it's possible for me to be. I don't think I'm always as humble as I ought to be. I'd like to be though, so maybe that's in my favor.

Well, Jesus Christ was over there on the mountain. And in the darkest of the night He was able to see. The Bible says He SAW them toiling in rowing for the wind was contrary. HE SAW THEM.

ARE YOU REALLY AWARE THAT GOD SEES YOU?

Maybe you're struggling with a temptation right now. Maybe you're on the verge of doing something that you will regret the rest of your life. Well, I want to tell you that He who loves you, and is able to strengthen you, sees the problem you're going through. God is aware of your temptation. And He's not being judgmental about it. He's ready to come to you in love to enable you to escape, so you will not indulge in that terrible experience which may destroy you or hurt someone else.

Jesus came down from that mountain because there was a terrible need these disciples had. Soon He was there at the point of their need.

Where are we to look for Christ?

We are to look for Him at the point of our need.

Try it sometime. Where do you have the greatest need? Think about Him. Ask, "Are You here? Are You really here, Lord?" And you will discover He is there. You will hear His voice.

> *Thine ears shall hear a voice behind thee, saying,*
> *This is the way, walk ye in it* (Isaiah 30:21).

Every time I quote that verse someone says, "How will I know it's God's voice? How will I know *God* is speaking to me?"

My answer is, "Nobody can tell you. I can only tell you you'll hear His voice. I can't tell you how or what form it will take, but God *will* speak to you. God will come to you and it will be a very meaningful thing to you. Simply be alert. And remember, God is concerned about you."

There Jesus stood on the water. When the disciples saw Him they were frightened. But one of them took a risk of faith. The fourth meaning that I see in this great miracle is:

4. THE POWER OF A SINGLE ACT OF LITTLE FAITH

Not an act of *great* faith but an act of *little* faith . . . faith that was even mixed with doubt. Later Christ said to Peter, "O ye of little faith, why did you doubt?" There was both faith and doubt . . . and usually there *is* both faith and doubt.

Don't let that trouble you too much. Don't be overly worried when your faith is so tiny you scarcely know you have any. You'd be amazed how much that little bit of faith can do . . . how big a building it can shake . . . how many lives it can change . . . how it can quiet the sea . . . how it can bring answers to prayers . . . how it can calm your heart . . . how it can bring healing.

Simon Peter looked and saw the same thing the others saw. He saw what appeared to be a ghost or spirit of the occult.

You see, that's where people go when they don't understand that the purpose of God is to do His mighty works among them—His works of giving them life and giving it more abundantly. When they don't understand and fail to recognize this is God coming to help them, then they may foolishly turn to the occult.

We are all spiritual beings. We're all religiously inclined. We're all apt to turn to something that is beyond the mortal senses because when we live on this level of the physical senses we get defeated too often. And we hope there's something out there that's undefinable but yet real enough to touch. The disciples saw something that looked like a spirit, or at least it appeared to them to be one. However, Simon Peter cried out, *"Lord,* if it be thou, bid me come unto thee on the water." In other words, Peter said, "If You're really the Source for my life, then tell me to come."

And Jesus said, "Come."

Can you trust Jesus as your Source? Can you come into an understanding that Jesus Christ can do ANYTHING . . . that Christ can make a way for you when there is no way?

"Come," Jesus said.

Really, Jesus said four things to the disciples:

    (1) "Be of good cheer."
    (2) "It is I."
    (3) "Be not afraid."
    (4) "Come."

Well, Peter came down out of the boat. When his feet hit the water it became a liquid pavement and he walked on the water. We're not told how many steps Peter took— maybe two, maybe three, maybe a dozen. Who knows? The fact is, he walked on the water and he was able to keep on walking until he got his eyes off Christ, his Source. Then, suddenly, he was right back where he began. He became afraid because of the roar of the storm and immediately began to sink. And he cried, "Lord, help me." It was a short prayer. (Someone said if Peter had prayed any longer he would have drowned!) But the Lord heard the three short words of prayer Peter uttered and stretched forth His hand and caught him.

Can you picture this in your mind? I wish some artist would paint it . . . Jesus standing there on top of the waves with one of His disciples who had walked with a little faith and had been able to get that far. Then he loses what little faith he has. He goes into doubt, he starts to sink, and he cries for help. Then Jesus reaches out His hand and catches him. In other words, Simon Peter is in the act of disappearing beneath the water but Jesus catches him with His hand and He pulls him up. And together they walk back to the boat and the wind ceased.

Now, you say, "Oral Roberts, is it possible that a miracle like this can happen to me today?"

Yes, it certainly is possible. The Bible says that Jesus Christ is the same yesterday, today, and forever (Hebrews 13:8). In a changing world, God changes not. In an impermanent society, God is forever permanent. It's a wonderful thought to know that in all the generations of man which have come and passed, God remains; and if Christ walked on the water then, which means that He prevailed over the storm, He walks on the water now, which means that He prevails over the storms of life now. And if He wanted a man to leave a sinking boat and come to Him, where the water was calm, and to be delivered from the storm of life then, **He**

wants you to be delivered from the storms of life today. I believe that.

When I was sick and afflicted with tuberculosis, it came into my heart that God could deliver me, that God could change my life and make something of it. And I praise the Lord today from the depths of my soul for the great changing power of the Living Christ. It takes a miracle. I know that. A miracle happened to me, but that miracle happened because I wanted it to happen. I wanted to be delivered and I wanted to use my faith and trust in God. Sure, I doubted some but I believed, too, and God really helped me. Jesus said, "Come, Peter. If you stay in the boat, you will sink. If you remain where the storm is, you will not survive; but if you will come to me, you too can walk on the water" . . . and he did!!

Friend, you can change your way of thinking. You can come out of that negative cycle of life. Christ is right. He says, "Come." Now do something about your situation. Focus your attention on changing things for the better.

Here are some things that you can do.

First, admit that your boat is sinking. Admit that you need help. Admit that Christ is right and that Christ can help you.

Second, understand that Christ wants you to come through this storm. He wants you to be safe, secure, normal and prosperous. Don't let the devil make you believe that God doesn't love you, that God does not want you to be happy. God is rich. God is healthy. God is happy. God has peace of mind, and God wants you to be all this too.

Third, get a point of contact. When Christ said to Peter, "Come," Peter made the

word "come" his point of contact. He
walked down out of the boat and just kept
walking. And when his feet touched the
water, the Bible says, he walked on the
water to go to Jesus.

Now, you cannot walk on the water unless you are going to
Jesus. You cannot have a miracle unless that miracle leads
you to God. You can change your life by a miracle through
your faith in God. Christ's miracle-working power enabled
Peter to walk. It took a miracle, but faith . . . even a little faith
. . . brings that miracle.

LISTEN:

When you think JESUS . . . think SOURCE.

. . . think FAITH.

. . . think MIRACLES.

. . . think HIS HAND
STRETCHING
OUT TOWARDS
YOU.

. . . think THE POWER
OF GOD FOR
YOUR LIFE.

. . . think CHRIST AND
MIRACLES AND
YOU GO
TOGETHER.

SUMMARY

WHATEVER YOUR SITUATION MAY BE TODAY,
KNOW THIS:

1. **All is not lost!**

Your problem may be too great for any human power
to solve but it is not bigger than God. And God is

there with you—at the point of your need—and He is saying, "I know how you feel and I am concerned. I LOVE YOU. And I can and will help you."

2. **Faith is in obedience.**

Obedience is in our faith and our faith is in our obedience. You have to have an obedient spirit. Your faith has to take action. You have to focus upon God and determine in your heart to do His will. Whatever God says to you (whatever you feel He is saying to you deep in your heart), do it!

3. **You can have a completed miracle!**

A completed miracle is a person with a thankful heart who knows he got more than he deserved. When your miracle comes—and it will—don't forget to thank God your Source for that miracle. You may find God through the need that you are facing right now. But when that need is met, don't stop there. Go on and make God the Source of your total life! Know that you now have Someone you can turn to at any time . . . anywhere. Cultivate a thankful heart.

8

HOW THE CONTINUING MIRACLES OF CHRIST CAN PROTECT YOU AGAINST THE OCCULT

PART 1

And they came over unto the other side of the sea, into the country of the Gadarenes. And when he was come out of the ship, immediately there met him out of the tombs a man with an unclean spirit, Who had his dwelling among the tombs; and no man could bind him, no, not with chains: Because that he had been often bound with fetters and chains, and the chains had been plucked asunder by him, and the fetters broken in pieces: neither could any man tame him. And always, night and day, he was in the mountains, and in the tombs, crying, and cutting himself with stones. But when he saw Jesus afar off, he ran and worshipped him, And cried with a loud voice, and said, What have I to do with thee, Jesus, thou Son of the most high God? I adjure thee by God, that thou torment me not. For he said unto him, Come out of the man, thou unclean spirit. And he asked him, What is thy name? And he answered, saying, My name is Legion: for we are many. And he besought him much that he would not send them away out of the country. Now there was there nigh unto the mountains a great herd of swine feeding. And all the devils besought him, saying, Send us into the swine, that we may enter into them. And forthwith Jesus gave them leave. And the unclean spirits went out, and entered into the swine: and the herd ran violently down a steep place into the sea, (they were about two thousand;) and were choked in the sea. And they that fed the swine fled, and told it in the city, and in the country. And they went out to see what it was that was done. And they come to Jesus, and see him that was possessed with the devil, and had the legion, sitting, and clothed, and in his right mind: and they were afraid. And they that saw it told them how it befell to him that was possessed with the devil, and also concerning the swine. And they began to pray him to depart out of their coasts. And when he was come into the ship, he that had been possessed with the devil prayed him that he might be with him. Howbeit Jesus suffered him not, but saith unto him, Go home to thy friends, and tell them how great things the Lord hath done for thee, and hath had compassion on thee. And he departed, and began to publish in Decapolis how great things Jesus had done for him: and all men did marvel (Mark 5:1-20).

I'M GOING TO SHARE with you two pages of an unusual letter written by an occult-bound daughter to her mother. The mother is a partner in this ministry and she sent a copy of her daughter's letter to me so I could know what she was going through and better know how to pray. In her letter the daughter said:

> Mother, I want you to know Christ personally so He can help you as He once helped me. Now

I'm hopelessly lost, which makes my desire for you to have God at your side even stronger. I've always had a strong obsession with the occult and several months ago I foolishly committed myself whole-heartedly to it. I cannot possibly get out—not now or ever.

I realize my past and present actions have hurt you terribly but you mustn't stake your own future happiness on anything I do or have done. I fully believe that within a year I'll either be in prison or dead. Either way I couldn't care less. I'm not the least bit afraid of dying even though I know what's in store for me. Hell couldn't possibly do anything to me that I haven't already done to myself.

The thing that grieves me most is what will become of my little daughters. Their very lives are at stake every minute they're with me, but I cannot bear being separated from them. They are in a foster home and they've been there for several weeks under police protection. But I told the police that everything was resolved in order to get them back. As long as I'm alive I want them with me because without them I have absolutely nothing, not even myself. That sounds strange, I'm sure, but it's true.

I've surrendered my very soul to Satan and there's no hope whatsoever of regaining it. I hope you'll always remember that brief time of peace and happiness we shared, and treasure it as I do. I'm not the daughter you knew then and never will be again. I've been in and out of jail for many serious offenses. I live from one pill to the next. I'm about as close to being an alcoholic as one can get. I've managed to conceal my desire for alcohol for quite some time now. (I always had a bottle in my locker at school and was known for drinking perfume during class.)

I'm not writing these things to hurt you, Mother, but I, too, am tired of our little charades. I feel you have a right to know. My therapist has even suggested shock treatments for some of my problems, but I refuse to submit to such drastic measures. Nothing short of a miracle could solve any of my difficulties. Since I belong to the First Church of Satan, I'm really not expecting one (a miracle)—not from God anyway.

I've shared this letter because it's indicative of a lot of mail that I get and a large number of people that I deal with through this ministry. They write me after watching me on television, or they hear about the Oral Roberts University and what we stand for, so they write and enlist our prayers. But in addition to that, I shared this letter that you might understand better the great miracle of our Lord in healing demon-possession—of casting out unclean spirits.

THE OCCULT IS AN EFFORT TO INVADE DEATH

The *occult* is described in the dictionary as being in the nature of something concealed, something that cannot be seen by the human eye, that is beyond the sense level. It is an attempt to go beyond the veil of that which we know is human into that mystery realm of the unknown.

As we know the occult in the Bible, it is demon-possession and demon-oppression. It's the work of demons in human lives. It is the work that the human eye cannot see . . . that the human senses do not experience in a direct way. It is concealed from that standpoint but it has an outward, very obvious and seeable, devastating effect upon the total personality of the individual. It also affects other people through that person.

I believe the occult is an effort to invade death. It is an effort to pull the veil back that separates the known from the unknown, the human from the superhuman, the five senses— the level of the five senses on which we live—from that level out there that's beyond the senses. It's an effort to communicate with those who have already died. That's one of its forms. The occult is also self-destructive.

With that background, let me talk about the man of Gadara who is otherwise known as Legion. The story is told in Mark 5 of how he was confronted personally by Jesus Christ.

DEMONS ARE FALLEN ANGELS

First of all, the man Legion was not insane. He was not mentally ill. This was not insanity in the terms that we know insanity. He had not suffered a blow on the head or there was not something congenitally wrong with his brain. This man was *indwelt by an unclean spirit.*

In the Bible an unclean spirit is described as a disembodied spirit who once had a body . . . who once was an angel. The archangel Lucifer led an uprising in heaven and was cast out by God to the earth where he was made the prince of the power of the air and the god of this world. The angels that followed him were also cast out and they lost their celestial bodies. They are now disembodied spirits. They are spirits without a body and they always seek embodiment in a human. (Read Isaiah 14 and Ezekiel 28.)

Now why do demons primarily seek to indwell man— man's body and being—rather than an animal. Because man is the only being made in the image and likeness of God.

Man has the widest powers of expression. He's the only one who has intellect and soul combined in one body. He's the only one through which a demon can fully express himself.

The expression of the devil is always to kill, to steal, and to destroy. How do we know this? Jesus Christ himself said in John 10:10:

> *The thief* (Devil) *cometh not, but for to steal, and to kill, and to destroy: I* (Jesus) *am come that they* (you) *might have life, and that they* (you) *might have it more abundantly.*

You can draw a dividing line between the devil and Christ.

On the one side is the devil stealing, killing, and destroying.	you	On the other side is Christ giving life and giving it more abundantly.

I think one of the greatest things in the world you can learn is that there is one dividing line and there are just two sides. There's the devil's side and Christ's side. On the one side is the stealing, the killing, and the destroying; on the other side is the giving of life and giving it more abundantly —and you are in between.

You can really divide this world into the good and the bad.

You can describe your personality as good or bad.

You can describe your inner nature as good or bad.

You can describe your actions as good or bad.

I know there are gray areas. I realize that. But in the final analysis you are a human being under God's control and guidance or one who is influenced and oppressed and directed by a satanic force.

It is Satan's purpose to steal from you, to kill you, to destroy you, to dry up the finer feelings you have within and to cause you to turn away from God and bind you until you cannot be delivered except it be by a miracle of Jesus Christ. Again I say I'm not talking about an insane man here, but I'm talking about a man who was indwelt by evil spirits.

What did the unclean spirit cause this man to do? It caused him to become *antisocial.* He turned against people. He was very nervous around a person or crowds. People turned him off so he left people and went to a cemetery. He had his dwelling there among the tombs. He had no meaningful relationships with human beings. And of course he had none with God.

WHEN ONE DOES NOT HAVE A MEANINGFUL RELATIONSHIP WITH GOD, IT IS VERY DIFFICULT TO HAVE A MEANINGFUL RELATIONSHIP WITH A HUMAN BEING.

This man had his dwelling—his life—among the dead. It's an obvious effort of his now to go beyond the sense level and communicate with the dead. He wants to penetrate the veil between the known and the unknown. He's turned away from God. He's turned away from people. Now there's nothing but that unseen world out there that is as real as we are. We human beings are real. Our Savior Jesus Christ is real. And the world of the devil and his unclean spirits is real.

CAN ONE COMMUNICATE WITH THE DEAD?

Is it possible to communicate with the dead? Of course not! Well, then, what happens when a person says he is communicating with the dead? I believe this is simply a demon or demons impersonating the dead. The Bible describes the devil as having the power to change himself, or transform himself, into an angel of light (2 Corinthians 11:4)—that is, to *appear* as a real or true angel. And that would be true of the unclean spirits or the demons who are under the authority of the devil.

So here we see Legion trying to transcend the level of the human senses and go into the unknown and reach out to those who have died, trying to find the meaning of his own existence—some purpose for his life. And also to invade death. I believe that the deepest purpose of the occult is to enable one to invade death. I believe at the heart of everything Satan deals with is death. He does not want to die or to cease to exist as he now does.

In a moment we will see that these demons, who are confronted with Christ and commanded to come out, beg Him not to send them into hell *before their time.* That is, there is a special time in history when God will consign every demon and the devil to hell . . . to a final hell. (Read Revelation 20:10-15.) Meanwhile, according to Jude 6 in the New Testament, they are contained in this world in chains of darkness. The chains are not literal chains. The chains are darkness . . . darkness of their mind . . . the lack of spiritual illumination. Those are the things that constitute their chains. And they are held without spiritual illumination in this world until they'll be put into the final hell.

Here the demons are begging Christ not to consign them to the final hell—even asking for the privilege to enter into an animal, even though the animal has no intellect or soul. The demons want embodiment so much that they are willing to enter animals.

The occult originates in the desire of the devil and his unclean spirits to take over the authority and power of God in the world . . . to pierce the veil between the known and the unknown . . . to go beyond the level of the senses and defy reality. For in going away from God they have lost their reality. They have lost their embodiment. They have lost their spiritual illumination. They are now described in the Bible as stars wandering, not knowing where they're going, having no home, having no embodiment, having no meaningfulness (Jude 13).

This man Legion had his dwelling among the tombs. He actually dwelt in that world of trying to constantly communicate with the dead world. The world that contains the spirits of people whose bodies have died. It's a frightening thought but that's what they're doing. He had an unclean spirit.

Legion was constantly in a state of self-destruction. Here Legion is in the tombs crying and cutting himself with stones. He is making sacrifices to appease the gods, which is a part of certain types of occult worship today. Sometimes they kill chickens or even snakes and use them in their satanic rituals. Sometimes they kill human beings for this purpose. Some of the murders that have been reported, where people were mutilated, were done by some of these people as a form of appeasing the gods. It is a part of their satanic worship. It is a part of their way to get through to the unseen world where they believe all reality is.

So Legion was in a state of self-destruction, of cutting his body, mutilating himself, and of course CRYING. The Bible suggests his crying was in the most deep-throated way. That is, the cries were coming out of the very bottom of his throat. He was mutilating himself. He was reaching out to the dead.

People had tried to tame him. That is, people had tried to bring him to his senses. And as the girl said in the letter I shared with you, she felt that since she had committed herself to the occult she was irretrievably lost. That is, she feels that she will always be that way. Here people in the community tried to deal with this man in a rational way—on the level of the senses—to restore him to society, to where he could be a people-loving person and could find meaningfulness for his existence.

This man's resistance was deeply rooted in his freedom of choice. He *chose* not to reenter the human world. They bound him with chains but he would break these chains. That is, they imposed the normal regulations of life upon him but they could not be successful because his mind rejected those impositions. His mind simply had a mind-set, a soul-set, a set toward the devil. And he would not relinquish that.

Maybe I can illustrate this by an experience two professional men had. One was a doctor and one was a lawyer. They grew up together as children. They went to grade school and high school together. They went to college together. They courted and married girls they both knew. They lived close to each other. They had their practices on the same street. They went to church and worshiped together. Years went by. One was a success, the other a failure.

They were together one evening and the man who had failed looked at the other and said, "I want to ask you why you've made such a success of your life and why God is so meaningful to you? I have become such a failure. God means nothing to me."

The friend went over and poured some liquor into a glass and set it down in front of his friend. He said, "I want you to watch me." He picked it up, put it to his lips, but he didn't drink. He set it down and said, "It's true we grew up

together and went to church together and prayed together.
I still pray and still go to church and still serve God. I've
reached a place, like my Lord, who could take up His life
and put it down. I can pick up that glass of liquor or I can
put it down. Now you pick it up."

The man who had failed, picked it up.

Then his friend said, "You've established a life-style to
where you can't put it down. You're using your power of
choice in the wrong way."

The man said, "Well, I can put it down." And with great
effort he did.

"Yes, but can you leave it there? Go ahead and pick it
up. Pick it up again," the friend urged.

The man picked it up. He was shaking and with blood-
shot eyes he lifted the glass toward his lips.

Then his friend said, "You asked the difference, here
it is. Our Lord could take up His life or lay it down. In the
same way, I can take that glass of liquor or lay it down. But
you can't. You don't have the will to do it and only God can
give you that kind of power."

A second time the man who had failed struggled to put
the glass down. Finally he got it down but you could tell he
didn't want to. He was bound to the habit of liquor.

Finally the friend said to him, "I want you to drink it."

The man was reluctant to do so, even though he wanted
to.

But his friend said, "I want you to drink it, and when
you drink it I want you to promise me something. I want
you to pray to it. I want you to acknowledge it as your god.
I want you to worship it."

And the man said, "You know I can't do that."

"Well," the friend said, "that's the thing you've given
your life to. So what you are doing is a form of worship.

Liquor controls you, so just promise me that you'll acknowledge it as god and you'll worship and pray to it."

That really got to him. The man set the glass down and said, "I'm going to choose. By God's help I'll make that choice today." And he did. He received a healing out of that experience. With God's help he conquered his desire for liquor and its control was broken in his life.

LEGION CHOSE TO BE WHAT HE WAS

Legion opened himself to the occult. How did he open himself? He opened himself by turning away from God, turning away from people, isolating himself and having no meaningful purpose for his existence. I have heard it said that if you can find the *why* of your existence, you can find the *how* to live it. But if you don't know the why, you'll never find the how. This man had lost hope, he had lost the reason for his being, and without it he could not survive. And there opened up a vacuum within him. Since he had refused God, Satan could come in and fill the vacuum with himself.

I think demons enter people through the person's own power of choice. Primarily because they have turned away from their Source, God. They've turned away from people and they've lost their meaning of existence. A vacuum is created and the devil has an open door. Really in that situation, the devil can't be kept out because the power of choice of the individual decides that that's what the person wants.

I've often thought about the Statue of Liberty in the harbor in New York. As the ships sail in from overseas the first thing they see is the great Statue of Liberty given to us by France. I've often thought that in addition to the Statue of Liberty, this country should construct a Statue of

Responsibility and put it on the West Coast. This would help balance this country so that freedom and responsibility for us would go together.

The man Legion had the freedom of choice. Through the freedom of choice he chose—he chose to open himself up to Satan. But once the devil got control and the legions took over—the many demons that divided his personality—he was absolutely hopeless.

How did Christ deal with him? He dealt with him in a personal confrontation. I believe . . .

CHRIST WILL HAVE A CONFRONTATION WITH EVERY HUMAN BEING AT SOME TIME OR ANOTHER

How did the confrontation come about? Christ came in a boat and just as He was landing, this man met Him. He screamed out at Him in a pseudotype of worship, "Jesus, thou Son of God." Legion worshiped Jesus but he wasn't worshiping Him any differently than he had worshiped the world of the dead, the spirits of the dead, or the devil. Jesus would have no part of that type of worship. Jesus dealt with him by speaking to the demons within him and saying:

Come out of the man, thou unclean spirit.

Then Jesus got to the key issue. He said, "What is your name?"

In that time the name of a person meant much more than it does today. The person often did not want to reveal his name because usually it disclosed his real identity. When Jesus said, "What is your name?" He was saying, "Who are you? Identify yourself. Admit what you are."

You know, that's the hardest thing for you or me or anyone else in the world to do . . . to admit *what* we are . . .

what we've done wrong . . . where we are wrong in our lives. That's very hard for us, isn't it?

Jesus was saying for him to identify himself. "Admit what you are . . . admit what you've done." And that took the power of choice.

The man had to exercise his freedom of choice. Finally he responded. He said, "My name is Legion, for we are many."

He was making a confession. He was saying, "I am divided in my personality. I'm divided in my being. I'm no longer a single entity or single personality. I'm divided, I'm torn apart. I want to worship God and I want to worship the devil. I want right and I want wrong. I want to go to heaven and I want to go to hell. I want to laugh and I want to scream. I want to live in town but I also want to live in the cemetery."

You see the mixed-up confused state he was in. He was actually many persons in one. The very key issue is: WHO ARE YOU? Jesus is asking everybody to reveal himself to himself.

Now in psychoanalysis they like for you to speak of your childhood or anything that comes to your mind . . . to simply speak out, even if it's something painful. And it is often something very painful to tell. By skillful direction and question-asking the analyst is often able to help a person. But that type of thing would not have any power or effectiveness in dealing with an individual like this. He did not need to go back and tell the painful experiences of his early life. What he needed was something stronger than that: HE NEEDED TO BE TOLD.

The major difference in being psychoanalyzed and in being "gospelized" is right here. Jesus Christ doesn't tell you to start relating all your experiences, no matter how painful they are, and then guide you with skillful questions until you can decide how to cure yourself. He simply indicates you cannot cure yourself of demon-possession. You cannot free yourself. The demon has to be spoken to, identified, and commanded by the power of God to come out.

Then finally Jesus dealt with him on a deeper level of his being. After He had freed him of the demons Jesus said, "I want you to go and tell the great things the Lord hath done for you."

I don't believe it's possible for anybody who's been delivered from demons or delivered from sin or any negative thing in life, to become a whole being without substituting in that place—the place of the old—a new mission in life. You cannot become a whole person without discovering the purpose for your being. Without becoming a seed-planter. Without investing yourself, giving of your love, giving of yourself, planting seeds of faith. Without opening yourself up to people.

Jesus commanded Legion to go back to people and to talk with them, to share with them. To give of himself. To redefine his mission in life . . . to enter into their needs. It's amazing how through this experience Legion, having been delivered and becoming a new kind of being, was able to change those people's minds and have them ready for Christ when He returned in His next visit (Mark 5:20).

Meanwhile, as Jesus was casting out the demons they wanted to go into a herd of pigs nearby rather than to be consigned to hell. Now there's been a question, too, through the years as to why Jesus allowed the demons to come out and then sent them into pigs—about 2,000 in number—which were worth a lot of money. Why did Jesus allow the property of some human being to be destroyed? I'd like to point out to you that the Bible does not say that Jesus sent them—the demons—into the pigs. It was the demons themselves who asked to go there. They said, "Don't send us to hell, permit us to enter the animals. Permit us to have some embodiment." The Lord gave them permission to do what they did. But the pigs could not contain them. The pigs had no intellect or soul. There was nothing for the demons to hang onto and so the pigs self-destructed.

Legion is cured. We see him clothed. He had been naked and now he has clothes on. He's sitting at the feet of Christ and he's in his normal right mind. He's saying, "Lord, let me go with You wherever You go." He received not only a deliverance from demon power but salvation.

This is a picture of our being in our right minds, dressing in a proper way to conceal our nudity, our nakedness, and saying to Jesus, "I want to be with You. I want to go wherever You go."

The Lord said, "I want you to go and to share. Tell the good news to your family and to your friends. Go back to your family and to your friends."

AN AMAZING TRUE STORY

Many years ago a mother gave birth to a baby boy and in giving birth to this baby, she gave her life. Although she knew she was dying, she expressed the thought that she felt she was giving to the world something in this child that would one day be of great benefit to many people. Therefore, she felt her death was not in vain.

This little boy grew up. At the age of eight and in the third grade, he was asked with the other students in the class to give an oral recitation. He was not exceptionally good in memorizing things but he had worked hard on this one and had learned it well. And when the time came for the recitations the mothers and the loved ones were invited to be there. Most of the children had their mothers or the various members of their family present, but of course this little boy's mother was in heaven. Nevertheless as he stood up to give his part he did very well until he came to the last two lines, and his mind went blank. And standing there in confusion, his face turning red, terribly frightened, he didn't know what to do except to stumble over and sit down. And all the little classmates, like children do, began to snicker and laugh. That he could take. But then all of a sudden the teacher laughed. And when she laughed something snapped inside him, and he later became what society calls a savage.

HATRED BREEDS CRIMINALS

A hatred developed in him toward human beings and by the time he was 12 years old he had become a hardened criminal. At the age of 16 he fell into the company of an international crook who had brought from India to the United States a very special type of criminology. It was an ingenious way of cracking safes. And this boy, who was now a teenager, became their student in crime. He was taught a way to sandpaper his right hand to the point where it would almost bleed. But just before the blood would ooze forth they would stop. And these master criminals that taught him learned that the force of their passions could be felt in their hands if they were sandpapered in this way. And when they planned a criminal act, they would hold up the hand that had been sandpapered to this degree and found that they could detect danger up to a mile away.

This young man was Starr Daily and by the time he was 20 years of age he was one of the most brilliant criminals that ever lived in the United States. He was one that probably never would have been caught but he made the mistake of taking up the habit of drinking.

INCORRIGIBLE

Eventually he was caught and pronounced incorrigible by judges and psychiatrists from coast to coast who had dealt with him, and Starr Daily spent all but three or four of the next 25 years behind prison doors and among them he was in four major prisons in the United States.

In the meantime Starr's father spent two or three fortunes trying to change his son. Finally the father, exhausted of all his money and feeling like he didn't have long to live, went to the warden and asked if he would let Starr come home for a day and let him be with him for just that short time. The warden granted the father's request. And in that brief period Starr's father tried to reach him, as he had tried to do through letters and visits for many many years. But he was unable to do so.

During this time he experienced all the tortures and devices to break his spirit that the prisons could dream up. He could not count the number of times he had been in the *hole* or starved or beaten. They had even hung him by his hands for days at a time until his flesh would become just a mass of bruises and sores. But Starr Daily learned one thing through all this—he learned that no matter what they did to him, if he hated enough he could endure anything they threw at him. And because of his intense hate, they were never able to break his spirit.

CHRIST'S LOVE BREAKS ALL BARRIERS

However, there was a brief period in his life before he was eight years old in his father's home that he had a very deep feeling about God. He had a love for Jesus Christ and he had recurring dreams about Jesus. He would dream that Jesus would come to him and he would see Him in a garden, always the same beautiful garden. And Jesus would be walking toward him and he could see Jesus' eyes full of love. On the other hand, he had two fears, one of death and the other of being held in a close place—claustrophobia.

Now as the months passed the father's heart was broken and he died. Then a strange thing happened the day that Starr Daily's father died. For 15 days they had been what they call "cuffing" Starr Daily in that they put his hands over a wall where they chained them and he had to stand there for 12-hour periods without food, without being able to go to the restroom or anywhere. And on the final day the warden, in a desperate effort to break his spirit, had the guards to beat him. They eventually beat him almost into unconsciousness. But because of his hate he wouln't open his mouth. He wouldn't make a sound. There was nothing they could do. Then just before he lost consciousness something happened and he forgot to hate. At that moment (he later learned) his father had died and in that same moment Christ came into Starr's life. And suddenly Starr had the dream he had when he was a little boy. He was back in the garden and Jesus was walking toward him and he saw the love in His eyes. And as Jesus walked toward him it was like a magnet pulling at him and it was like the sun was being focused upon him, drawing out the hate, the poison, the bitterness, the criminal tendencies which had never been conquered. At that moment the doctor stepped up and said to those who were beating him, "Don't hit him again." He turned and said to the warden, "Put him in the hospital." And the next few days various women would come in and bring him things to eat.

He later discovered these were the wives of the guards who had beaten him.

And then as he got well the doctor asked that he be assigned to him so he could teach him to become an anesthesiologist. And Starr Daily was now so infused with love that it was like Jesus Christ was actually possessing not only his being, but also He was physically present. There was something coming forth from this man that you could feel and it was a positive, life-giving force.

So he became the doctor's aid and during the weeks and months he filled the hospital areas wherever he was with the feeling of love he had in his heart. And the doctor never lost a patient while Starr was his male nurse.

One day they brought in a man from the prison and the doctor said, "I cannot operate on him because I believe we have only one chance in a thousand of being successful in the operation."

And Starr Daily said to the doctor, "Doctor, do I understand you right, that you have only one chance in a thousand?"

And the doctor said, "Yes, that's right. I don't want to tackle it."

And Starr Daily said, "Do you have one chance?"

He said, "Yes, we have one chance."

He said, "Doctor, is it possible that you would let me take the responsibility for that one chance?"

And the doctor agreed.

And while the doctor was doing the surgery, Starr Daily stood at the man's head and looked at the doctor's hands throughout the operation. But he never saw the doctor's hands. He saw only the hands of Jesus Christ. And he poured his love in like the sun pouring through a piece of paper until the paper catches on fire. When the operation was over the doctor said, "It is a success." Then he took off his mask and said, "I'm going to my office and I don't want to be disturbed." And there in his office he gave his life to Christ and was converted.

A WAY OUT

Meanwhile, Starr Daily was changed from his cell to the cell of an old "lifer," a man who had been in prison for some 40 years and had gained his freedom but had returned. And because he had met Christ he wanted to spend his last days in the prison to witness where he could. He was a very quiet man and it wasn't long until he had gained the respect of the inmates, the guards, and the warden.

When Starr Daily became his cellmate and the old lifer began to give him some advice, he said to him, "Starr, you are in here for life, but if you ever get a parole, what would you do? And Starr said, "I'd like to be able to write and to talk, to communicate with people."

So the old lifer suggested that Starr go to the warden and ask permission to take a correspondence course. At that time in this country, they didn't have an educational system such as is now in the prisons of the United States, and the warden turned him down. So back in his cell, Starr began to send his love toward the warden. He visualized the warden in his office and he poured out his love toward him. And one day the warden called him and said, "Starr, I've decided to let you take the correspondence course you wanted," which he did.

So Starr began to write and to sell stories to well-known magazines. Then he realized what a great help this would be if other inmates could be educated while serving their time. And he asked the warden if it could be done and the warden turned him down. So Starr just kept focusing his love upon the warden. And one day a word of knowledge came to Starr. And he asked for an audience again with the warden and shared with him the thought of instituting correspondence courses and building libraries in prisons to rehabilitate prisoners so that when they had served their time they could come out useful citizens. He also suggested to the warden that America would always remember him as the warden who revolutionized the prison system in this way. And the warden bought the idea.

LOVE OPENS PRISON DOORS

But here is the final thing that has had such a tremendous effect upon me. One of the members of the parole board, even though he had heard of the transformation of Starr Daily, said, "As long as I'm on this parole board Starr Daily will never be paroled. He is one man in that prison that is incorrigible."

Well, this had almost a devastating effect upon Starr until the old lifer said, "Starr, love him."

And so Starr began to build imaginary funnels in his mind through which he poured his love. He built these funnels to send through the prison and down the streets and over the hills and through the town to where this lawyer lived. And every day he would send his love through these imaginary funnels.

One day the lawyer picked up the phone and called the warden and said, "Warden, I don't know why but I've changed my mind. I'm ready to vote to let Starr out." And Starr was released from that last prison. And for the rest of his life he was a force to change the prisons by changing some of the systems under which they lived. Starr said that

he had never known a prisoner to change and to be transformed except by the love of Jesus Christ. He said, "He cannot be reformed, he can only be transformed."

You know, when I think about this the question keeps
coming to my mind, *why don't people want God?* Why don't
people love people? Why don't we look up and catch a
glimpse of that love that's greater than any love and reach
out for it? Once we have experienced even a little bit of God's
love, we will want to focus it upon people, upon persons,
upon events, upon needs.

FOR SUMMARY, SEE CHAPTER 9, PART 2

9

HOW THE CONTINUING MIRACLES OF CHRIST CAN PROTECT YOU AGAINST THE OCCULT

PART 2

And one of the multitude answered and said, Master, I have brought unto thee my son, which hath a dumb spirit; And wheresoever he taketh him, he teareth him: and he foameth, and gnasheth with his teeth, and pineth away: and I spake to thy disciples that they should cast him out; and they could not. He answereth him, and said, O faithless generation, how long shall I be with you? how long shall I suffer you? bring him unto me. And they brought him unto him: and when he saw him, straightway the spirit tare him; and he fell on the ground, and wallowed foaming. And he asked his father, How long is it ago since this came unto him? And he said, Of a child. And ofttimes it hath cast him into the fire, and into the waters, to destroy him: but if thou canst do any thing, have compassion on us, and help us. Jesus said unto him, If thou canst believe, all things are possible to him that believeth. And straightway the father of the child cried out, and said with tears, Lord, I believe; help thou mine unbelief. When Jesus saw that people came running together, he rebuked the foul spirit, saying unto him, Thou dumb

*and deaf spirit, I charge thee, come out of him, and
enter no more into him. And the spirit cried, and rent
him sore, and came out of him: and he was as one
dead; insomuch that many said, He is dead. But Jesus
took him by the hand, and lifted him up; and he arose.
And when he was come into the house, his disciples
asked him privately, Why could not we cast him out?
And he said unto them, This kind can come forth by
nothing, but by prayer and fasting* (Mark 9:17-29).

*And Jesus said unto them, Because of your unbelief:
for verily I say unto you, If ye have faith as a grain of
mustard seed, ye shall say unto this mountain, Remove
hence to yonder place; and it shall remove; and nothing
shall be impossible unto you* (Matthew 17:20).

IN THE AREA OF MEDICAL HELP, which I salute and am in
firm favor of, psychosis is defined as the deeper form of
human erratic, bizarre, or destructive behavior. There are
three main types: schizophrenic, paranoid, and manic depressive.

A schizophrenic would be the type of individual who
would withdraw and lose contact with reality. He'd be
"out of it," in other words.

A person who is paranoid would have delusions of being
someone else, maybe. He might think that he is Napoleon
or Jesus Christ or some other individual. I think you may
have encountered such people as these. They are unable to
accept themselves or to think of themselves as the person
they really are.

The manic depressive person has severe ups and downs.
He has a tendency to destroy—either himself, or someone
else, or something. He has this terrible feeling of destruc-
tiveness. When a person like this is down—when he feels

the mania or the depression so deeply—he can feel rejected, he can feel perhaps he has even blasphemed the Holy Spirit, or he may feel like killing himself. He has suicidal tendencies.

Without our great clinics and hospitals and the help of doctors, these three main types would be loose in our society. I would presume that most of them—at least the more violent ones—are either in clinics or in hospitals or institutions which are state and government supported for that purpose.

I wanted to point that out because I think the average Christian does not realize the great work of humanitarianism and compassion and medical skill that's being carried on for these types of individuals.

On the other hand, I think there are a great many Christians, especially at this time, who think that all such types of behavior are caused by demon-possession. I believe some of it is but I do not believe that most of it is. When a person is demon-possessed he is indwelt by another personality. An individual can be a schizophrenic without being indwelt by another personality. He can be paranoid without being indwelt by a demon spirit. He can be manic depressive without having a demon.

Now I am grateful for every kind of help that people receive. But what I'm going to talk about is our Lord Jesus Christ and how He dealt with a type of need that *seems* to be the kind that the medical profession would call schizophrenia or paranoia or manic depressive.

The first thing I want to address your attention to is that Jesus Christ has just been upon the Mount of Transfiguration where His former glory was revealed. That is, it seems that whatever He has been veiled in has been removed momentarily and the glory of His inner self shines out. His face shines above the brightness of the sun. There He is . . . luminous. His disciples—the three that went with Him: Peter, James, and John—are astounded as they see Him. Then Moses and Elijah come and speak with our Lord. It happens there on a high mountain. And it's called the Transfiguration. Our Lord's inner being, as it was before He was born a man, shines through His physical being—through his five senses. And it's a glorious sight indeed. It apparently doesn't last very long. But it was so glorious that Peter, James, and John wanted to stay there the rest of their lives.

Meanwhile, the other nine disciples remained at the foot of the hill. They were approached by a father with his son. The boy appears to be a teen-ager. And the father says he has a demon. The father calls it a dumb spirit. He says that this demon tears his son's flesh and throws him into the fire and into the water in an effort to destroy him.

We see here that the indwelling demon has been cut off from his Source. Now I'm going to use that phrase, *cut off from one's Source*, several times in this chapter.

We're going to see that the demon is cut off from his Source, who is God.

We're going to see that by indwelling the boy, the demon has also cut the boy off from his Source, who is God.

We're going to see that the father, through the practice of his unbelief, is cut off from his Source.

Then we're going to see that the disciples, through their unbelief, are cut off from their Source.

We're going to see how valuable it is to look to God as the Source—that God is the Source of your total supply.

When you are cut off from your Source, then it's like someone has strangled you or has done something to you that has caused your behavior to become erratic, unfamiliar, bizarre, and so unlike God. It's like you are from some other planet, cut off from your original Source.

DEMON SPIRITS ARE FALLEN ANGELS

I want to say that an evil spirit, a demon spirit, has been cut off from his Source. He's been cut off from God. He's an angel that has lost his body, his spiritual illumination. He was cast out of heaven because of his rebellion against God. He followed Lucifer who became the devil, who rejected God, rebelled against God, and tried to be God. The devil and his angels are now in the world but they've lost their bodies. Now they seek human embodiment because man has the widest powers of expression. Man has a soul. He is a worshiping creature. And the only way this disembodied spirit can strike back at God, whom he hates, is to enter a human being and to put within him his own characteristics to fulfill himself. Therefore, he has to reach out and try to possess that life. If he can get inside another life he can express his personality, his hate of God, his hate of humanity. Insomuch as he is able to do that, he gets some momentary sense of fulfillment until that last moment when he will be cast into hell. But he's cut off from his Source and his place and order in God's universe.

THE DEVIL COMES TO DESTROY

A demon has entered this boy and has remained in him through the years; he has changed his behavior patterns—in body, mind, and spirit. He has cut the boy off from his Source . . . so that his own vital life forces are being destroyed. He is being thrown into fire and into water with the purpose of destroying him.

Think of the devil in terms of John 10:10 where Christ said:

> *The thief* (devil) *cometh not, but for to steal, and to kill, and to destroy.*

That's why the devil comes. And the demons are his agents. The agent (demon) comes as the devil personified to enter a human being with the purpose of destroying that individual or using him to destroy others. In this case the demon is only trying to destroy the one individual. He's tormenting the boy's parents through it but the boy himself is being destroyed. He's gnashing his teeth. He's foaming at the mouth. He's being thrown to the ground. His mind is not functioning in a normal way. As I indicated, the vital life forces are being dried up. They are being destroyed until the boy is becoming a vegetable.

Now the father calls upon Christ to have compassion and if He has any power, to use it to help his child.

Notice that Jesus did not blame the father for his son's condition but He did deal directly with the father's own present belief, which was antisocial, or anti-God. The father himself had not been living the kind of life he should have lived. This was not the cause of his son's illness, but the father himself was in a bad state. His spirit wasn't right. And Jesus dealt with his condition. Christ looks at the father, at the crowd, and at His own disciples who have tried and failed and He says, "O faithless and perverse generation" (Matthew 17:17).

This is an indictment of human society as a whole, including the religious world. Jesus is saying, "You are faithless. You have built your religion not around faith, but around something that's institutional. You've got a theory of some kind but it is not based in faith and the Living

Lord. And you are perverse. You are perverted. The feelings that you were created with—to love one another—you've lost! The world is divided, not because people are physically divided but because in your innermost beings you don't like each other. You don't love each other. You don't feel compassion for one another. You don't experience faith in behalf of one another."

This is what Christ is saying. He's saying it to His own disciples. He's saying it to this father. It means this father has cut himself off from his Source. He has no Source for his life. And the disciples have cut themselves off, too, from the same Source—God. While they're trying to cast the demon out, Christ is upon the mountain. He's physically up there. Not only is He physically up there but also, as far as the disciples are concerned, He is not in *spiritual* contact with them either. They are cut off both physically and spiritually from their Source, who is God. Therefore, they are unable to cast this demon out.

DEMONS RECOGNIZE JESUS AND FEAR HIM

Immediately when the demon in the boy sees Jesus, it goes into action. I know in dealing with cases similar to this that the demon is so intuitive that when I have talked with these people before praying for them, sometimes they would finish my statement before I said it. This is the demon within the person who has this knowledge. I've often walked up to one of these individuals who was brought to the crusades and kept in the automobile for safety purposes. The person would have his head down and his eyes closed and when I'd walk up behind the car—without the person having any idea I was approaching—I would hear him screaming my name. I remember one case where the demon was saying, "Oral Roberts is right behind the car. Now he's beside the car. Whatever you do, don't let him touch you. Don't let him touch you with his right hand."

This person's head was down so he could not have seen me. I had a friend with me, a layman I love very much. When he saw what this demon was doing and saying, he started to take off. I grabbed him and said, "Come on, this will do you good."

Then I reached into the car and as I did the demon said, "His right hand is coming toward you. Don't let him touch you." Now can you imagine a person sitting there with his head down, eyes closed, having this kind of knowledge without seeing or hearing?

The demons KNEW.

It's like Acts 19 where there were seven sons of a man named Sceva who were trying to cast out demons. They came to a man possessed of demons and said, "In the name of Jesus, whom Paul preacheth, we cast you out."

And the demons said, "Jesus we know, and Paul we know, but who are you?"

Then the man, in whom the devils were, leaped upon these seven men and tore their clothes off. And the Bible says, "They fled out of that house naked and wounded" (Acts 19:16).

Later the disciples wanted to know why they could not cast the demon out and Jesus said that this kind could not come out except by prayer and fasting. Jesus spoke of their unbelief. That is, Jesus said you've got to have faith as a seed that you plant, then you can speak to this mountain.

Jesus began to talk about Seed-Faith.

First, you have to be connected to your Source—God is your Source.

> **Second, you have to be in a state of compassion and love,** or a state of giving to people.
>
> **Third, you have to have an expectation that the seed you plant will become a harvest . . . will become a miracle . . . from God. That's what the disciples did not have.**

I feel that Jesus Christ's statement, "faithless and perverse generation," coupled with His statement, "You have not been fasting and praying," meant: "You have not made your faith as a grain of mustard seed. You have not planted seeds of faith. You've not tied yourself to your Source."

Jesus' technique in casting out this demon appears to be simplistic. But I don't think it is. It *appears* to be because He makes it a simple issue. He says, "You have a demon . . . thou demon, come out!" The facts are:

First, Jesus actually addressed the demon. He ascertained how long the demon had been in the boy. He learned that the demon had come into the boy when he was evidently small—at a young age. Now he's apparently a grown young man.

Second, Jesus called this demon a deaf and dumb spirit and said, "Come out, come out, come out!"

Third, Jesus said, "Enter him no more." He apparently put up a shield that the demon could not pierce in the future.

Matthew 12:43 says that when a demon comes out of a man he walks through dry places or uninhabited regions —that is, regions uninhabited by man—and he seeks rest. That is, he seeks embodiment. But if the demon cannot find it he returns to the person from whom he has been cast out, *with seven others.* If he can overpower that same man, then the last state of that man is worse than the first. In other words, when the demon is cast out he tries to find embodiment somewhere else. If he fails he returns to his home base. This is why I think Christ said, "Enter him no more."

When I pray for the people to be delivered from demons I always end the prayer by saying, "And enter him no more, in the name of Jesus Christ of Nazareth." I'm just using the technique that Jesus used.

But when you study Jesus' approach, listen to His statements, and see exactly how He does it, you begin to see that it's a comprehensive view of the entire individual. It's the whole man view. It's a direction of God toward the entire personality of the individual—his body, mind, and spirit.

I firmly believe that the best part of medical treatment can be traced directly back to the life of Jesus Christ. I believe that the deepest meanings of usefulness that we have in philosophy in our whole world can be traced back to the Bible and to the teachings of God.

I want to tell you right now that exorcism is nothing for a group of uninformed people to get involved in—to go around trying to cast out demons.

In the first place, not everything is caused by a demon. I know there are some people who think every kind of strange behavior is caused by a demon. Well, it's not! Some people are just mean! Some people are just terribly sinful. A demon is an indwelling personality and you've got to have some experience, some contact with God, a divine calling to cast it out. I think it's really a divine calling. I don't think just *anybody* can do it. Maybe they can. I'm for it if they can, but I just give a little word of warning.

DEMONS TRY TO RESIST THE POWER OF GOD

The demon was striving *not* to come out. He resisted the power of God.

Sometimes even in conversion we see people resisting God and their bodies contort. They're not in a state of perfect obedience where they can relax and let the Holy Spirit bring them into the kingdom of God.

Well, this is true in a deeper sense in this case. When the demon came out he actually tried to kill the boy. He threw him to the ground. The boy, after suffering from the violent hold the devil had upon him, seemed to be dead. But Christ just gave him His hand. He picked him up and restored him to life and to his father.

Suddenly, the boy is free by the power of God.

SUMMARY FOR CHAPTERS EIGHT AND NINE

1. All mental illness is not demon-possession—know the difference.

2. Demon spirits are fallen angels looking for embodiment.

3. Demons recognize Jesus and fear Him.

4. Know the purpose of the devil is . . .
    to kill . . .
    to steal . . .
    and to destroy you.

5. Know God's purpose is . . .
    to give you life . . .
    and to give it more abundantly.

6. You have the power of choice to will yourself to God or to the devil.

10

HOW THE MOST DIFFICULT MIRACLE OF CHRIST EVER PERFORMED FOR ILLNESS AND PROBLEMS CAN HELP YOUR MOST URGENT NEEDS

After this there was a feast of the Jews; and Jesus went up to Jerusalem. Now there is at Jerusalem by the sheep market a pool, which is called in the Hebrew tongue Bethesda, having five porches. In these lay a great multitude of impotent folk, of blind, halt, withered, waiting for the moving of the water. For an angel went down at a certain season into the pool, and troubled the water: whosoever then first after the troubling of the water stepped in was made whole of whatsoever disease he had. And a certain man was there, which had an infirmity thirty and eight years. When Jesus saw him lie, and knew that he had been now a long time in that case, he saith unto him, Wilt thou be made whole? The impotent man answered him, Sir, I have no man, when the water is troubled, to put me into the pool: but while I am coming, another steppeth down before me. Jesus saith unto him, Rise, take up thy bed, and walk. And immediately the man was made whole, and took up his bed, and walked: and on the same day was the sabbath. The Jews therefore said unto him that was cured, It is the sabbath day: it is not lawful for thee to carry thy bed. He answered them, He that made me whole, the same said unto me, Take up thy bed, and walk. Then asked they him, What man is that which said unto thee, Take up thy bed, and walk? And he that was healed wist not who it was: for Jesus had conveyed himself away, a multitude being in that place. Afterward Jesus findeth him in the temple, and said unto him, Behold, thou are made whole: sin no more, lest a worse thing come unto thee (John 5:1-14).

I WANT TO SHARE with you on the miracle of the healing of the whole person. This may be the most difficult miracle of healing that our Savior ever wrought. There were so many contributing circumstances to this case that it took the best of God and the best of the man to bring this miracle to pass. It is the only one of its kind that is explained in detail in the New Testament. Here we have some information about the way Christ works in the healing process that we don't have in any other place in our Lord's recorded life.

Here we have a multitude of sick people who have gathered because of a story that they've heard concerning a pool of water in the city of Jerusalem. According to the legend, the waters were stirred up at a certain season by an angel. The first person who stepped into the water while its waters were boiling up was made whole of his disease. That single incident in which one human being might be healed had caused a multitude of sick people to congregate.

Now doesn't that say something about the human race, about the human individual? The need of healing has always been so great that people will virtually go to any length and submit to almost any kind of process in order to obtain a cure. Now I can't deprecate that because I believe God put in us the desire to be well.

Never shall I forget my discovery in 1947 of a verse in the New Testament which I should have known a long time before, because I had studied and read the New Testament over a hundred times. The verse is in the little book of 3 John. It says:

> *Beloved, I wish above all things that thou mayest prosper and be in health, even as thy soul prospereth* (3 John 2).

That was a grand occasion for me because I'd always been taught that it might or might not be the will of God to heal. Yet in the midst of that we had doctors practicing medicine, who were doing their best to stamp out disease. The very religious people who wondered about God's will to heal would go to a doctor and try to get healed. It was a paradox to me why they would separate healing into medical and spiritual healing. Why not just combine them and give the glory to God for any or all of it?

This verse—3 John 2—means a great deal to me because it wrapped up the healing process in a single entity of making a person whole. It showed that . . .

THE VERY WISH OF GOD IS THAT A PERSON PROSPER, THAT A PERSON HAVE HEALTH, AND THAT HIS PHYSICAL HEALTH BE EQUAL TO THE HEALTH OF HIS SOUL. IT IS GOD'S WISH FOR A PERSON TO HAVE A WHOLE MIND, A WHOLE SPIRIT, A WHOLE BODY, AND WHOLE FINANCES.

It meant God wanted a man to prosper, to be able to live and meet his needs, to pay his bills, and have his needs met so he could be a whole person as he goes through life and someday meets the Lord.

About that same time, I discovered John 10:10. When I say *discover*, I don't mean I hadn't read it before but it had not leaped out at me and become so clear in its meaning. In John 10:10 our Lord said:

The thief (devil) *cometh not, but for to steal, and to kill, and to destroy: I am come that they* (you) *might have life, and that they* (you) *might have it more abundantly.*

This verse had a striking impact upon me. I'd been a young man who was once terribly ill and had gone through the process of sickness. I also had borne the theological discussions about sickness which finally resulted in my minister's saying to me, "Son, be patient." Had I been patient I would have been dead today. Hearing people talk about how it might be God's will for me to be ill . . . and asking what I had done to cause all this . . . or saying, "God has your number" . . . or "God made you ill" created some very grievous and grave doubts in my mind about God's goodness. I think when I finally received Christ as my Savior, was filled with the Spirit, and healed, this enabled me to discover and to say to the world some things that I think are very important, such as:

GOD IS A GOOD GOD!

GOD LOVES YOU AND CARES FOR YOU.

GOD WANTS TO MAKE YOU A WHOLE PERSON.

I know that doesn't sound very new today but in 1947 there weren't many people talking like that. It meant a lot to me. It strengthened me because I was almost alone in my thinking as I went from place to place in the crusades. I drew large crowds but controversy swirled about me all the time. I had to face a lot of things that were said about me that were not true. I still have critics today but not nearly so many as then. I think in some respects it was good because it made me really learn the Bible. It made me study the life of Jesus. It forced me to lean upon the Holy Spirit. Above all, it made me examine myself to see if I really believed what I was preaching.

When criticism and opposition come toward you, you can take it and make it a force with which you examine your motives. Another thing criticism will do for you is find your weaknesses. Your friends won't do that. Only your enemies will find your weaknesses. If you're sincere and you want to be the kind of person God wants you to be, you can take that. For if you do have a weakness, you want to try to be strong rather than weak. I don't have a lot of the weaknesses I had then, because my enemies very carefully and sometimes cruelly pointed them out and I plugged them up as much as I could. Some, I couldn't plug up. Some, I'm still plugging on.

THE BEGINNING OF A LIFE-CHANGING DREAM

In Enid, Oklahoma, in 1947, the Lord's time had come for me to enter the ministry of healing. This was a ministry I knew little about except the fact that I'd been healed myself of tuberculosis and healed of almost all my stammering when I was 17.

It was a lonesome time. I knew my time had come and I didn't know what to do or where to turn. I had a dream night after night. Each time the dream would awaken me. And each time when I was awakened by the dream, I was not in bed; I was walking in my house. I'd never walked in my sleep before but I had this dream night after night, and it was always the same. In the dream God was letting me see people as He sees them and hear them as He hears them. To my astonishment I saw that everybody in the world is sick. I didn't know that. But I saw that within each person there is a cry, a moan, a sigh. And I heard that moan and cry and sigh. Then I saw the love that Jesus had for people and that love touched me. I fell in love with the sick. I remember having all kinds of experiences with the sick in my dream and later in reality. And I still have that feeling with me today about the sick that I can no more escape than I could escape breathing. I'll have this feeling till I die.

I dreamed I saw the human race as God sees them and as God hears them and as God loves them. I knew I'd never be the same again because I saw that:

EVERYBODY IS SICK IN SOME WAY. EVERYBODY IS MOANING, SIGHING, AND CRYING INSIDE ABOUT SOMETHING THAT'S HURTING HIM.

I now know that Jesus loves every person. I now *know* that. And there are times that I have that kind of love in a greater degree. I wish that I could have it more. So I was reminded of the sighing, crying, moaning multitudes that I saw in my dream as I read of this great multitude of sick folks around the pool . . . and Jesus was in their midst. I hope that's something you will never forget:

THE NAMELESS MULTITUDES, LIKE MASSES OF UNCOUNTED ANIMALS, ARE SO DEAR TO OUR LORD THAT HE'S IN THE MIDST OF THEM.

There the multitude was surrounding the pool . . . grasping at a straw, knowing that out of their vast number only one could conceivably be healed. That is, if this tradition were true and the angel troubled the water, still only one person would be healed. Yet they were so desperate for a cure, they waited.

Christ selects one of them. It's evident to me by the reading of the whole passage that He dealt with more than one but I believe this one is recorded because it is an example of what He does with all sick people. If we could see behind the scenes we would see Jesus dealing with us along the same lines that He dealt with this man.

Jesus found a man who probably would be described today as being *psychosomatically* ill. A psychosomatic illness is one which, more or less, springs from the emotions. It's not organic, in other words. This kind of illness is so often dismissed with, "Oh, it's only psychosomatic! It's *only* that!" But this kind of illness just happens to be about the hardest thing in the world to deal with because there isn't a surgeon's knife in all creation that can cut it out. There isn't anything on this earth that can deal with the innermost depths of a human being but the Spirit of God. This is why, in my opinion, that:

NOBODY IS EVER FULLY HEALED, REGARD-LESS OF HOW SUCCESSFUL HIS SURGERY MAY BE OR THE MEDICINE IS, UNTIL GOD HIMSELF IS IN ON THE CASE AND THERE IS A COMBINA-TION OF THE HEALING FORCES COMING TO-GETHER.

They're all important. None of them is unimportant. Now I have a tremendous respect for organic disease. I have a tremendous respect for psychosomatic disease. I mean respect to the extent that I recognize them both and I know that they are strong. I also know that a doctor sometimes can treat an organic disease much easier than he can treat a person who is psychosomatic in his illness.

I want you to notice something else—Jesus did not deal with the man's sickness. He dealt with the man who had the sickness. And in dealing with the man who had the sickness He was also dealing with the sickness.

For example, say you have a cancer which is caught in time and can be cut out. You may undergo successful surgery but that doesn't mean you have necessarily dealt with the trauma that is going on in you—the human individual out of which that cancer has been cut. The trauma of the whole experience is still there and the stress it puts upon a person is often devastating.

I've come to realize that I cannot always tell the difference between organic and psychosomatic illness. And most doctors I talk to say that they're not always sure themselves, but that they can get pretty close.

The fact of the matter is that our human life is so complicated it's virtually impossible for anybody—a minister, or a doctor, or anyone else—to say with absolute accuracy that a certain disease is organic or psychosomatic. Doctors can give the same medicine to two people with the same disease. It may work on one and not work on the other. Surgery will work on some people and won't work on other people.

We can pray. We can pray for the healing of people who have the same illness. Some get healed and some don't.

So here is a man whose condition is so complicated that we have no words to describe it. We simply have to accept it as a fact. This man had been there ill for 38 years. That is to say, he had been coming there to the pool for 38 years. At that time he had been enduring this infirmity of his flesh and spirit. The Bible describes him as impotent, which would mean in his case that he was now out of the picture. He was useless. He was ineffective. He was no longer "with it" at all. He was carried to the pool on a bed, a little pallet. There he lay with the other sick people surrounding the pool. For 38 years he had attempted to get into the water, and for 38 years he had failed.

By the time he meets Jesus Christ he's full of bitterness and he's blaming the other people for getting in ahead of him. He had a *single* idea of recovery and that was to be the first one to get into the water. He had tunnel vision. It was like he was looking through a tunnel and all he could see was that little pool of water and waiting for the moment it boiled up, hoping he'd get in first. It was not reliable . . . 38 years of unreliability had been his.

It's just like today when we get our mind on one thing and that's the only thing we think that is going to help us. We get our mind on one particular method . . . one method and that's it! For example, suppose I'm facing surgery and I think if the surgery doesn't do it, there's no other help. Or, if I have a particular person to pray for me and I think, if he doesn't get through for me then nothing is going to help. This is a tunnel-vision kind of thing. It's turning to the instrument and making it the source.

GOD USES MANY INSTRUMENTS.

IF ONE INSTRUMENT DOESN'T WORK, GOD HAS ANOTHER.

I've never said anything more important in my life about healing than what I've just said. There's a vast difference between a source and an instrument. And if you or I get our minds upon one thing other than God himself and make that our source, we're making a dreadful mistake. What if that fails us? Then we're crushed. We become disillusioned. There are people walking around on this earth, or they're bedfast, or behind prison bars, or in hospitals, who had one way to go. It failed them and now they are without hope. They're aimless. They have no meaning in their existence and it's like they are dead already.

It's like you get up in the morning and you don't want to get up. You don't want to wash. You don't want to comb your hair. You don't want to put on your clothes. You don't want to go to work. You don't want to go through the day. It's a day of boredom and when night comes you want to get through it. You dread for the next day to come and then you dread the next night. We are walking dead people because we have lost our hope.

Do you realize that the thing the doctors fear the most is this? This can cause more surgical failures than anything else. So many people go into surgery and it is not successful because they don't go in there with a meaningful, positive, believing attitude that this, too, is God's work. They don't go in there with faith.

The same is true when we receive prayer. If we don't go into it with a meaningfulness, with a positiveness, it will not be successful. One of my difficulties in praying for people is that they don't often calm down or stop talking long enough to have prayer. I mean, they're so full of the problem. I can understand that because I've done the same thing. When I have a terrible problem I'm so full of the problem that when someone's trying to help me with the answer, all I want to talk about is the problem. I become problem-centered and not answer-centered.

THERE'S A TIME TO LISTEN

Not long ago I prayed for an individual who was just talking so fast and furious and so hysterically that I did something that would appear to be an insult. I just simply told her to stop talking. I mean, I'd been nice. I'd tried to calm her down and finally I said, "Stop talking!"

Then I said, "Do you want to be healed?"

And again she started telling me everything in the world.

Well, I know it's important for us to get things out of us, but the trouble with that is if that's all we think and talk about then we are never going to get out of it. So I said, "Ma'am, please don't open your mouth again. You came a long way to receive prayer and now you won't let me pray. Now go on your way or let me pray for you." That's a hard thing to say to someone, but it's also a hard thing to have a knife put across your stomach and to go through surgery. It's hard when you are growing up to have your mother or daddy slap you across the cheek or take a strap to you, but sometimes you need that. You need someone to look you in the eye and say, "Listen, it's time for you to shut up and listen for awhile." If we really want help, let's quit messing around with our lives.

Personally, I wouldn't go to a doctor if I wouldn't listen to him. If I didn't intend to try to do what he told me to do, I wouldn't go. And I wouldn't go for prayer unless I was willing to do what the person felt led for me to do.

Anyway I found this person was really gracious. When she realized what she was doing she stopped and said, "Brother Roberts, I'm sorry. I've been through a lot but I realize I am dwelling on the problem. Do help me."

I said, "Now then you put me in a position where I can help you." I put my hands on her and her body was trembling. The gift of God works through me and I'm grateful. I don't always say it like I'm saying it now but what usually happens is that the Spirit flows through my hand and when I take hold of a person, I know a lot. I don't know it unless the Holy Spirit is moving through me, I'll tell you that. But I picked up what her problem was and I told her. She nodded yes, and that gave her confidence.

And I saw what I call a miracle. I don't know that others would call it a miracle, but I saw a woman calm down. She was no longer hysterical, with a desire to say all those things she'd been saying. She was now in control of herself. She could look at me and talk in a conversational tone. She was calm. She was ready to leave and she was happy.

Now I don't know what people call that but to me that's a miracle, or doing the works of the Father. To get any one of us human beings that calm and that rational, in my book, is about the hardest miracle in the world.

HEALING BEGINS IN THE INNER MAN

Well, this man had been there by the pool with his illness for 38 years and Christ is beginning to deal with him. The Bible says that He knew. Jesus *knew* and He asked him a question, "Wilt thou be made whole?"

It's a silly question from our standpoint—"Wilt thou be made whole?"

"Well, certainly! Certainly! Why do you think I'm here?" we would say. Well, this man didn't understand the question either.

Jesus said, "Wilt thou be made whole?" He said that after He had seen him *lie there*. The Bible did not say He had seen his body lying there, though that was obvious. Jesus saw his body but now He's talking about the entire person. He's talking about the man *inside* the body. He's talking about the inner self. He's talking about that central core of our existence. With divine love Jesus grasped the central core of the man's existence and said to him, the *whole* person, "Wilt *thou* be made whole?"

Jesus was going all the way back to creation when God breathed in the man's nostrils the breath of life and he became a living soul. God placed the inner man inside the body so that the inner man is the man with a body wrapped around it. We bury the body but we never bury the man. We just take the physical flesh out and bury it. But the man, the inner man, leaves the body. If he's a saved man he goes straight to our Lord. It was Paul who said that to be absent from the body is to be present with the Lord (2 Corinthians 5:8). Otherwise, if a person does not know Christ his soul goes to hell (Matthew 25:41).

Jesus saw something that nobody else saw. The crowd saw a man lying there with a sick body. Jesus saw a man inside the body lying down. And He knew that was bad. Oh, that was really bad. Now there's where it's tough to get a miracle. So Jesus said, "Will *you* be made whole?"

And the man said, "Well, Sir, I have no man to put me in the pool. Every time I try to step in another steps down before me. For 38 years I've been defeated."

You see, he didn't understand the question. Jesus was not talking merely about the healing of his body—though He included that. Jesus was talking about the healing of the whole person. The man was now full of bitterness and blaming others, which is the most natural thing we humans do.

Do you often find people who will take responsibility? Do you often find a person who will say, "Yes, I did it." "Yes, I'm mean." Did you ever hear anybody say, "I'm jealous." "I'm envious!" Did you ever hear anybody say, "I cheated . . . Yes, I lied." "Yes, I stole that." "Yes, I slipped around behind your back and told a lie on you." "Yes, I did it."

"Oh," the lame man said, "I didn't do that—not me, no!"

There isn't a person who has not been lied on, stolen from, put in a bad light or hurt by somebody. And stored up within you and me is some form of bitterness. Big or little, it's there and it's affecting us. The result is our body is losing its immunization against certain types of disease.

I know it affects me like that. You let me get down in my
spirit, down in my inner man, and my body virtually goes
to pieces. And contrariwise, when my spirit gets up I can
do great things.

For example, for some time I have had a goal of run-
ing two miles without stopping. This is part of my personal
aerobics program. And I wanted to run that two miles
within so many minutes. Not long ago I achieved my goal
of running two miles without stopping. I want to tell you
how I did it. I'd been defeated for three months because my
spirit would get down. It takes about twelve and a half laps
on the track in the ORU Aerobics Center to go two miles.
I'd get up to eight laps and nine laps and my spirit would
quit on me. Suddenly my body would not run. I couldn't
get one foot in front of the other. I finally got up to ten of
those laps and I thought I could go on and get my two miles
but my spirit quit on me. I mean it quit and lay down. So I
would stumble off all sore and stove-up.

But the day came when I got up to ten laps. Now I
was within reach of my goal so I said to myself, "Self, smile.
Every step, smile! Enjoy this! You can do it! You can do
it!" I was having me a time. Every now and then some girl
would swish by and then a boy would swish by. The students were out-running me on all sides. But they should,
they are younger than I am. Well, there I was—only two
and a half or three laps to go. And I got the old inner man
standing up. He quit lying down on me. And do you know,
when I finally made the two miles I could have gone another lap or two, easily.

I said to myself, "Self, you really learned something
there." Instantly, I was reminded of Matthew 26. It tells
of Jesus in Gethsemane. He had gone through the struggle
of facing the cross and finally He said to his disciples, who

were asleep, "Rise and let us be going." RISE. They were lying over there asleep and they were lying down inside. He said, "Rise, get up."

And that leads me to the next statement. Jesus said, "Wilt thou be made whole?"

SPEAK TO YOUR INNER MAN

And then He said, "Rise, take up your bed and walk." Jesus spoke the word to the inner man, not to the body because the body cannot rise in itself. There isn't a person who can stand up unless his will tells him to do it. Try. Go ahead. You can't do it. Your outer man cannot function unless the inner man tells it to.

"Rise, stand up on the inside."

Say it. "Stand up on the inside."

Jesus said, "Take up your bed. You've been lying on it. It's been supporting you. Now you pick it up and throw it across your shoulder. Instead of it possessing you, you possess it."

I dealt with a mother who had had terrible struggles in her marriage and her family for about fourteen years. As she told me, I could tell that she felt like I do sometimes. She was lying down on the inside. I told her she was and I said, "Stand up in the inner woman."

And she said, "I don't want to stand up in the inner woman."

I said, "Well, that sounds bad but it's a good confession."

You know, if you feel that way, say it and get it out of you so that you *can* stand up.

One man said to me, "Mr. Roberts, my problem is this: I love God but I don't like people."

Another man I started to pray for, left me. He just turned and ran away. Then a couple of days later he came back. (This happened at one of the crusades.) He said, "I guess you wonder why I ran off?"

I said, "Yes."

He said, "Well, as I stood there, I remembered a certain wrong I had done that I needed to fix up and make right. So I fixed it and I'm back. And I know God's going to do something in my life."

I could see it in his eyes. I could see that the inner man had stood up and shown him that it was not merely a physical problem we were dealing with, although it was physical. We were dealing with a whole person.

"Rise, take up thy bed and walk." You know what? The Bible says, "And he was made whole." He was made whole.

Adam was *created* a whole man and lost it through disobedience.

Jesus Christ was *born* a whole man and kept it through obedience.

But this lame person was *made* a whole man.

One was created, one was born, and one was made.

And I believe that Jesus Christ can make you a whole person.

Now the final thought is this: Jesus immunized him against this recurring. He said, "Go and sin no more, lest a worse thing come upon you." This is to say, the behavioral pattern of this man was sinful in the eyes of God. God counted the blaming of others, the bitterness, the treating of himself merely as a physical being as a sin. The man lying down on the inside was sinful. For He said, "Go and sin no more, lest a worse thing come upon thee."

That is, Jesus was saying, "The worse thing will not come upon you. I will immunize you against this same type of impotence if you will go and sin no more."

Or, in our language Jesus was saying, "If you'll stand up on the inside . . . if you'll recognize that you are a person and not just a mere human body . . . if you'll just keep on rising and standing up on the inside and keep on taking up your bed and keep on walking—if you will rejoin the human race, you will be made whole!"

The miracle of the healing of the lame man was one of the roughest ones Jesus encountered And it took the best of God and the best of man to accomplish it.

SUMMARY

THIS MIRACLE SAYS TO YOU IN THE NOW:

1. **God is a good God.** God loves you and cares for you. God wants to make you a whole person.

2. **Everybody is sick in some way . . .** and none is completely healed regardless of how successful his surgery or medicine may be, until God himself is in on the case and there is a combination of healing forces coming together.

3. **God is the Source of all healing.** He uses many different instruments. If one doesn't work, God will use another instrument.

4. **Healing begins in the inner man**—you must WANT to be well.

11

THE MIRACLE
OF THE POINT OF CONTACT AND
HOW YOU CAN USE IT TO RELEASE
YOUR FAITH FOR MORE MIRACLES

*And when Jesus was entered into Capernaum, there
came unto him a centurion, beseeching him, And saying, Lord, my servant lieth at home sick of the palsy,
grievously tormented. And Jesus saith unto him, I will
come and heal him. The centurion answered and said,
Lord, I am not worthy that thou shouldest come under
my roof: but speak the word only, and my servant shall
be healed. For I am a man under authority, having
soldiers under me: and I say to this man, Go, and he
goeth; and to another, Come, and he cometh; and to my
servant, Do this, and he doeth it. When Jesus heard it,
he marvelled, and said to them that followed, Verily I
say unto you, I have not found so great faith, no, not in
Israel. And Jesus said unto the centurion, Go thy way;
and as thou hast believed, so be it done unto thee. And
his servant was healed in the selfsame hour* (Matthew
8:5-10, 13).

*And when Jesus was passed over again by ship unto the
other side, much people gathered unto him: and he was
nigh unto the sea. And, behold, there cometh one of the*

rulers of the synagogue, Jairus by name; and when he saw him, he fell at his feet, And besought him greatly, saying, My little daughter lieth at the point of death: I pray thee, come and lay thy hands on her, that she may be healed; and she shall live. While he yet spake, there came from the ruler of the synagogue's house certain which said, Thy daughter is dead: why troublest thou the Master any further? As soon as Jesus heard the word that was spoken, he saith unto the ruler of the synagogue, Be not afraid, only believe. And he cometh to the house of the ruler of the synagogue, and seeth the tumult, and them that wept and wailed greatly. And when he was come in, he saith unto them, Why make ye this ado, and weep? the damsel is not dead, but sleepeth. And they laughed him to scorn. But when he had put them all out, he taketh the father and the mother of the damsel, and them that were with him, and entereth in where the damsel was lying. And he took the damsel by the hand, and said unto her, Talitha cumi; which is, being interpreted, Damsel, I say unto thee, arise. And straightway the damsel arose, and walked; for she was of the age of twelve years. And they were astonished with a great astonishment (Mark 5:21-23, 35, 36, 38-42).

For I have received of the Lord that which also I delivered unto you, That the Lord Jesus the same night in which he was betrayed took bread: And when he had given thanks, he brake it, and said, Take, eat: this is my body, which is broken for you: this do in remembrance of me. After the same manner also he took the cup, when he had supped, saying, This cup is the new testament in my blood: this do ye, as oft as ye drink it,

in remembrance of me. For as often as ye eat this bread,
and drink this cup, ye do shew the Lord's death till he
come. Wherefore whosoever shall eat this bread, and
drink this cup of the Lord, unworthily, shall be guilty
of the body and blood of the Lord. But let a man exam-
ine himself, and so let him eat of that bread, and drink
of that cup. For he that eateth and drinketh unworthily,
eateth and drinketh damnation to himself, not discern-
ing the Lord's body. For this cause many are weak and
sickly among you, and many sleep (1 Corinthians
11:23-30).

WHEN I WAS TRAVELING through America and the world
preaching to large masses of people in auditoriums and in the
big tent, I had to discover a way for the individual, in that
great mass of people, to reach out to God as a person. The
Lord enabled me to discover what I call the *Point of Contact.*

I'm extremely happy to share with you something that
you can use seven days a week for the rest of your mortal
life. It is called . . .

THE POINT OF CONTACT

All power has a point at which you make contact. In
your automobile you turn on the key or step on the starter
and the motor turns over. Or if you flip a light switch there
is an instant contact with the powerhouse that causes the
power to come singing through the wires to give you light.
The point of contact is made with the power that causes the
motor to come on.

There has to be a point of contact. The light switch, the
accelerator in your car—any source of power you can name—
must have a point by which you make contact with it. The
important thing is not the point of contact. The important
thing is that you release the power. The power is the thing

that you want released. So we put the point of contact in its proper context of usefulness. It is not an end in itself but it's a very useful *instrument* that was even allowed by our Lord Jesus Christ.

I'm going to talk about three points of contact used while Jesus was in His physical, limited body when He lived as a human being on the level of the five senses that we have: sight, touch, smell, taste, and hearing. Then I'm going to deal with one point of contact that was used when Jesus was beyond the sense level, in His present glorified form. I think you can use this point of contact—or any one of these, or others—every day of your life. They are tremendously important to you.

SPEAKING THE WORD IS A POINT OF CONTACT

The first point of contact I want to discuss is the one we read about in Matthew 8—*speaking the word*. It is about a Roman captain, not what we'd call a religious man, who had a very definite need of healing for his servant. Eventually he had to go beyond the emperor's physician, the army doctors, and come directly to Christ himself. Now it was a very, very great step of faith that he took because the Romans were ruling over Palestine. The Romans and Jews did not fraternize or have anything to do with each other. As a matter of fact, the Romans laid heavy burdens upon the Jewish people. So it was a very unpopular thing among the Romans for one of their number to fraternize with a Jew, particularly from a religious standpoint. Caesar was believed to be a god by the Romans and they called him "Lord Caesar."

But suddenly something takes place in the captain's life, where he called Jesus Christ "Lord." Now that was a dangerous thing to do because he's switching his allegiance from not only the commander in chief of the Roman armies under whom he had his appointment as a captain, but also from calling him lord and from bowing down to him as a divinity, to a lowly Nazarene—Jesus of Nazareth—who was a Jew.

The captain did it because, first, he had this need that could not be met by any other power that he knew about.

Second, the captain had come to realize that Jesus was the embodiment of life itself. So he came to Christ.

The very first word that came from his lips was "Lord." He'd never called any man lord before, except Caesar.

Then he bowed. He'd never bowed to any man before, except to Caesar. And as he bows there in the open street, bowing before Jesus Christ, it's a really dramatic scene. It is force bowing to meekness . . . armed might before the un- armed . . . the proud uniform of war before the seamless robe. He's bowing before Jesus, calling Him Lord, and tell- ing Him about his servant lying at home sick of the palsy, being very deeply tormented by the disease.

Christ responded immediately and said, "I'll come and heal him." That's a remarkable phrase of our Lord, "I will come and heal him." I truly believe that Jesus Christ was always on His way to heal someone, or He was there healing the individual, or He had just been there and the person was up and well, praising God.

I believe that Jesus Christ came to take off you what the devil put on you . . .

     and to put back in you what the devil took out . . .

     and to put back on you what the devil took off.

I BELIEVE THAT!!

Jesus said, "I will come and heal him."

Then the man said, "No, no, it's not necessary for You to come to my house where my servant lieth ill. It isn't necessary at all because, Lord, I'm a man under authority also. I know what authority is. You don't have to come. You just speak the word. Why, I speak the word and men obey my voice. They carry out my orders. Caesar is in Rome and he speaks a word of authority and I obey it over here in Palestine. I, in turn, speak a word to a soldier and he does what I tell him. So You don't have to come to my house. You just speak the word and my servant shall be healed."

And Jesus said, "I've not found faith like this even in the nation of Israel, where it's supposed to be."

Jesus indicated that . . .

FAITH IS WHERE YOU FIND IT

Sometimes you find faith where you don't expect to find it. Also when you look for it in places where you expect to find it, faith isn't always there.

Then Jesus said to the man, "You go your way, and as you have believed, it shall be done unto you."

Here's the commanding power of faith when it is released. The point of contact was "SPEAK THE WORD."

Why?

Because this is a man who recognizes authority and power. Up till this hour he had thought Caesar represented the very zenith of authority and power. Now he recognizes that Jesus Christ has authority and power above that of Caesar or anybody else. So he says that God has the greatest authority and power. Therefore, for him his point of contact was a spoken word from the Lord . . . just a WORD FROM JESUS. He did not require Him to touch his servant, or to go over there in person. He simply said, "Speak the word . . . Lord, let me hear You say it and I will believe."

That's why Christ said, "As you have *believed, it* shall be done." Remember Jesus did not say, "As I've *spoken the word,*" He said, "As you have BELIEVED."

What happened when Jesus spoke the word?

It became the point of contact that the captain's faith had with God. The Source of power for the healing of his servant was God but the captain had to have a point of contact with that Source of power. He was unable to release his faith unless he had some point of contact.

THE POINT OF CONTACT HELPS YOU TO REALIZE GOD AS THE SOURCE OF ALL POWER

What does the point of contact do? The first thing it does is to recognize God. It recognizes Him as the Source of all power. The second thing is . . .

THE POINT OF CONTACT SETS THE TIME FOR THE RELEASING OF YOUR FAITH

The point of contact sets the time. Now how? If I were to say to you, "I'd like to meet you."

And you say, "Fine, Oral Roberts, when?"

And I say, "Oh, any time."

And you said, "Where?"

And I said, "Oh, anywhere," you and I would never meet.

But if I said, "I will meet you."

And you said, "Where?"

And I said, "In front of the United States Post Office in downtown Tulsa."

And you said, "When?"

And I said, "Tomorrow at 3 p.m.," we would be setting the time and place so that all of our interaction would be used toward getting to that point at the appointed hour. You see what I mean? It's very important to set the time for anything you do. So the point of contact sets the time for the *releasing* of your faith. It doesn't set the time, necessarily, for the healing or for the miracle to happen. It sets the time for the *releasing* of your faith.

Now you can do several things with your faith. One of them is to just keep your faith inside you. And it'll never do you much good. One man said to me, "I have all the faith in the world."

"Well," I said, "why are you coming to *me* for prayer?" Then I said, "That's really your trouble."

He didn't understand. He said, "What do you mean, that's my trouble, when I tell you I have all the faith in the world?"

I said, "The trouble is you still *have* it."

He said, "What are you trying to say?"

"I'm trying to say to you, it isn't enough to have faith, you have to *release* it."

A person can have all the money in the world and still starve to death. We read in the paper every now and then where a recluse starves to death and $50,000 or some other large sum of money is found stuffed in a mattress in the room. In the same way, what's the use of having faith unless you release it? Now you can keep your faith—it's really inside you. You have it but it's doing you no good. Or you can release your faith. In the extremity you might even lose your faith.

Not many people lose their faith. You may hear a person say, "Oh, I lost my faith" but that's just a figure of speech. If you've really lost your faith, you've gone into apostasy. To really lose one's faith is, first of all, to have had it. Second, to have used it in Christ. Third, to have turned away from Christ. Not only turned away from Christ but also to apostatize, to blaspheme, and to believe that Jesus is no longer the Son of God. You declare Him to be something other than the Son of God—then you have lost your faith.

Not many people have really lost their faith. When a person says, "I've lost my faith," he's not saying that he has apostatized. Ordinarily he's simply saying, "I've not been using my faith," or "I've not been releasing my faith," or "I'm discouraged."

It isn't easy to lose your faith.

Someone says, "Well, how do I know I have faith?" Because the Bible says you do:

> *God hath dealt to every man the measure of faith* (Romans 12:3).

God has a certain measurement of faith and that measurement of faith is given to *every* man. Now you might not use your faith. What Christ is seeking is for you to *release* your faith. I used to say, "Turn your faith loose." That means, "Release it."

FAITH HAS TO BECOME AN ACT

What must faith become?

An act.

For example, in order for you to have faith in a chair you have to *act* on your faith and sit down in the chair. For your faith to be useful it has to become an act. You have to act on it. That is to say, you must release it.

The Roman army captain had faith in Jesus' authority and power so much so that he placed Christ's authority and power above Caesar's, above that of anyone else in the world. But even that was not enough. He had to act on that. And for him to act on it, he used the point of contact of having Christ say the word. The moment Christ said the word the man simply turned and went home. When he arrived he found the servant was healed. The point of contact did not heal the servant. But the point of contact helped the captain release his faith. He set the time to release his faith. What was the time he set? The moment Jesus spoke the word his point of contact released the power of God and his servant was healed.

So now what's the meaning of "the speaking of the word?" This point of contact works best for people who believe in the authority of Christ, that He's not only their Savior but He's their LORD. He's the Lord of their life and He's the Master over every situation that they'll ever face.

You see, there are many people who believe that Jesus Christ is their Savior and that they're going to heaven, but they don't really exercise their faith on a practical level. They don't really accept His authority over disease, fear, demons, poverty, or their bad circumstances. They just simply accept Jesus' power to save their souls by forgiving their sins and making them new creatures and taking them to heaven. And it's good they have that much faith.

But there is something beyond that, where you accept Christ not only as the Savior but also as the Lord and Master over your earthly circumstances. Even over your diseases, or your circumstances that are filled with bad things. Where you KNOW that the Lord has a way . . . and He can make a way where there is no way. It's a practical level of living daily under the mastership, the lordship, of Christ where you see that everything of a negative nature must yield to Christ. You never say, "God can't do that." You never say, "That's impossible." You cut the word *impossible* out of your dictionary. You come into a relationship with Christ till you believe that Christ is all and that Christ can do anything!

One of the great statements of the whole Bible is in the book of Job. The book of Job has 42 chapters. In the very last chapter, second verse, Job says:

I know that thou canst do every thing.

Even while Job said that he was sitting there with a terrible affliction in his body. His family had been killed. His wife had turned against him. His friends had turned against him. He was sitting there all alone in the world wishing he were dead. But finally he came to a point of faith that not only did he believe in God, but also he believed in the lordship of God. And he said, "God, I know thou canst do everything." At that very precise moment, God turned all those bad things away, healed him, and restored to him twice as much as he had lost.

This particular point of contact, having the Lord speak the word, is best used by people who believe in the lordship of Jesus—not only as their Savior to take them to heaven but also in His lordship in their lifetime.

Sometimes we say people get so heavenly minded they are no earthly good. You know, they're always thinking, someday God will take me to heaven. Well, I'd like for Him to take me around on the earth awhile first . . . to come into my house . . . and be with me in my automobile . . . and be with me in my career . . . and in my body that I have to live in 24 hours a day. I like for Christ to be in every part of my existence. I'd like to know that Christ can do everything and anything.

THE LAYING ON OF HANDS AS A POINT OF CONTACT

Now the second point of contact we shall discuss is the laying on of hands. This was used by Jairus, a ruler of the synagogue of the Jews. He may not have been a rabbi but he was a leader in the synagogue. He had a very responsible position in the house of God. Well, his little daughter became so ill that she came to the point of death.

Now it was a little difficult for such a man to come to Christ, just as much as it was for a Roman army captain to come to Him. The Roman army captain of course didn't fraternize with the Jews, so it was difficult for him to come.

But the Jewish leaders never did fully accept Jesus Christ as the Son of God. Some of them believed He was a prophet or a teacher, but they did not accept Him as the Messiah. So it was difficult from a religious point of view for a leader of a synagogue to come to Jesus Christ.

The Jews believed in the personhood of God. That is to say, they believed that some day the Messiah would come, and they are still looking for Him. One of the great reasons they have returned to Israel—returning from virtually all the nations of the world—and are rebuilding that nation, is that they believe in the Messiah. Now they may not say that. They may not even know that's why they came back. But many of them do *know*, and that's why they came back.

During my trips to Israel, in talking to hundreds of people from both high and low levels of society and even the former Prime Minister Ben-Gurion, I've never met anybody who did not say something about the Messiah. Either a person believed that the Messiah was coming or that He was a person. Some believed that it was Israel, but most people I talked to believed it was a person. Certainly the prophets in the Old Testament believed that the Messiah, the Anointed One, would be a person.

So here is a man who is making God a person. Jesus Christ represented to him the personhood of God. His point of contact, therefore, had to do with Jesus' hands. So the laying on of hands is best used by an individual who is more influenced by a person, who wants to feel the warmth of another person, who wants the intimacy of that kind of human contact.

Jairus said, "Come and lay thy hands upon my little girl that she may be healed and she shall live."

Jesus responded. When Jesus arrived the little girl had apparently died, but because the point of contact was made prior to her death and the man held on to his point of contact—never giving up—Jesus did lay His hands on the little girl and she revived.

This point of contact—the laying on of hands—set the time for Jairus to release his faith. While he and Jesus were on the way to the little girl's bedside some people met them and said to Jairus, "She's already dead; why trouble the Master any further?"

And Jesus immediately said, "Fear not, only believe and she shall be healed."

That is, **"Keep your point of contact! Don't turn loose of it.** You wanted the laying on of hands and that's your point of contact. Hold on to it."

Your point of contact may be the laying on of hands. It's been a point of contact for me, as well as the spoken word. I know that I've used both of them. One is just as important as the other.

Speaking the word was used by the apostles. Paul was preaching one day when there was a cripple in the crowd and he looked out and saw him. Paul saw the faith that he had and cried, "Stand upright on thy feet" (Acts 14:10). That's all Paul said: "Stand on thy feet." That's the spoken word. He spoke the word and this crippled man responded to that type of point of contact. He leaped and walked.

Well, the same man—Paul—used the laying on of his hands while on the island of Melita and great healing came to masses of people (Acts 28). This was during one of his journeys to Rome.

So various points of contact were used in the New Testament. The particular one used was usually in context with

the background of the person who needed the healing power
of Christ. In other words . . .

>GOD LOVES YOU SO MUCH THAT IN A SENSE
>HE ACCOMMODATES HIMSELF TO THE WAY
>YOU RESPOND.

And the thing that will help you establish your point of
contact is usually honored by God.

I remember something happening years ago when I was
preaching on the radio (which I'm still doing). I would tell
people to lay their hand on the radio as a point of contact
while my prayer was going out. I asked them to "just put
your hand on the radio and pray with me and use that as
your point of contact and release your faith."

Well, one woman was so ill that as she walked toward
her radio she couldn't reach it. She was there in her kitchen
and she grabbed onto the refrigerator to keep from falling.
She said, "God, I can't reach my radio; will You let this
refrigerator be my point of contact?"

Well, you know, the first thing you'd say is, "That isn't
going to help her."

Well, it did! I have her letter and she told of the remarkable way Christ came to her and gave her a healing as
she held on to that refrigerator. You see, that became her
point of contact. She set the time and released her faith.
It was her faith that made contact with the power of God
and brought the healing to her body. It was God's power
that did the healing—not the refrigerator, not even the
touching of it.

TOUCHING THE HEM OF JESUS' GARMENT
AS A POINT OF CONTACT

A third point of contact was used by a woman who
touched the hem of Christ's garment. Now to what type of

person would this point of contact be most applicable? It would be more applicable to a person who *images* what God is going to do in his life. For example, this was a woman who had been ill a long time. She couldn't get well, although she had spent all of her money on physicians. She was no better, but worse. I mean, she is at the end of her rope. In other words, she's out of money. She's out of health. It's about over and she hears about Jesus. So she says in her heart, "If I can but touch the hem of His garment I shall be made whole." She didn't say, "I'll be *healed*," but instead "I'll be MADE WHOLE."

The woman had an image in her mind of becoming a whole person, and that Christ could do it. She held this image in her mind. One sometimes becomes what he images himself to be.

When she came into the crowd it was too big for her to have an audience with Jesus. She couldn't get Him to *speak the word*. She couldn't get Him to *lay His hands* on her so she just simply reached out her hand and touched Him. She brushed her hand against the clothes of Jesus and instantly this was her point of contact. She released her faith.

At that moment Jesus said, "Somebody has touched Me."

She touched His clothes—she thought—but she actually touched Him.

And He said, "Who did it?" And everybody denied they had. In fact, everybody was brushing up against Him and touching Him. He said, "But I felt it! This touch was different because the healing power went out of Me."

When she saw that she was discovered the woman rushed up and said, "I did it."

He said, "Well, you go in faith, daughter; thy faith hath made thee whole."

Again, notice that the point of contact did not heal her.

It was her faith. But her point of contact was instrumental in her healing. It was the touching of His garment which set the time for her to release the faith she had that would allow her image of being whole to come true.

THE HOLY COMMUNION AS A POINT OF CONTACT

The fourth point of contact that I wish to discuss briefly with you is the Holy Communion discussed in 1 Corinthians 11:23-30. Our friends in the Episcopal and Catholic faiths call it the Mass or the Eucharist. The word "eucharist" is really a derivative of charisma, one of the gifts or graces of God. It really means great thanksgiving. It's a vertical thing from your heart, going up to God.

The Protestants call it Holy Communion, communion of the saints, communing with one another. So it is both a eucharist and a communion. It is both a vertical praise to God for His sacrifice upon the cross and it is a horizontal communion with one another. It is a faith in Christ and a love toward the brethren. So in a sense, both terms are beautiful and highly useful.

When you come right down to the Holy Communion, it has, through faith, not only great power to deal with your soul but also with your body. It is indicated here in 1 Corinthians that some of the Corinthians who were taking the wine and the bread were not grasping the meaning of our Lord's Body. They were just eating and drinking without faith and they were missing what it was all about. The sicknesses they had were not being healed. Some of them were dying before their time. That is, they were not taking advantage, through faith, of the bread and the wine. They were not grasping the meaning of the Body of Christ, first, in that they were not looking up to Him in great thanksgiving. And, second, they were not grasping the meaning